CHARACTER AND CRIME
An Inquiry into the Causes of the Virtue of Nations

Michael Novak

Brownson Institute
Notre Dame, Indiana
1986

Distributed by arrangement with
University Press of America, Inc.
4720 Boston Way
Lanham, Maryland 20706

Modern Catholic Library 1

The First Aquinas Fund Lecture on Responsible Citizenship sponsored by the International Society for Criminology.

Given at the School of Philosophy, Catholic University of America, Washington, D.C., October 8, 1985

Permission, for which the author is grateful, has been granted to reprint James Q. Wilson's "The Rediscovery of Character," *The Public Interest,* 81 (Fall 1985). An abridged version of the title essay was published in the Spring/Summer 1986 issue of *This World.*

The Brownson Institute
Post Office Box 1006
Notre Dame, Indiana 46556
(219) 234-3759

For my mother and my father,
Michael J. Novak, Sr., and Irene Sakmar Novak

Table of Contents

Preface
by Giacomo Canepa *

As president\ of the International Society for Criminology, I wish to express my gratitude to the School of Philosophy of the Catholic University of America and to its Dean, professor Jude P. Dougherty, that have organized and hosted the First Meeting of our Society's Aquinas Program for Criminology on "Responsible Citizenship."

Criminology, the interdisciplinary science of deviant and antisocial behavior, has been particularly affected by the present crisis of human sciences. This crisis manifests itself not only in the clinical field but also in the sociological one.

Analysis of the historical evolution of criminology shows that situations of crisis usually arise following the contrast between the actual requirement of a concrete renewal and its ideological contamination. In the history of criminology this has happened at least twice during the last hundred years.

At the time of the positivist revolution there appeared the need for a real renewal, aimed at the foundation of a "new criminology" (Garofalo), not based exclusively upon the consideration of the criminal action as a "juridical abstraction" but engaged, above all, in studying the personality of the man who committed the crime. This need was nevertheless contrasted and strongly opposed because it was considered the expression of an ideological prejudice which denied human freedom

7

(positivist determinism and biological determinism).

At the time of the sociological revolution there arose the need for a real renewal, directed towards the establishment of a "new criminology" whose activity was not limited to the study of the delinquent as a "biological" individual (antipositivist thesis) but which would mostly concern itself with considering the numerous social and cultural aspects of the environment in which man dwells.

In this case, a fair exigency met with a strong opposition because it was considered the expression of an ideological prejudice inspired by even more serious forms of determinism (social determinism). This interpretation was favored by the development of many sociological theories based exclusively upon the consideration of the social (and political) aspects, whilst attaching no importance whatsoever to man as an individual personality.

This situation has been very clearly exposed in the work of Taylor, Walton, and Young, whose very precise critical analysis is not only directed against the individualistic theories but also against the sociological ones. This criticism, however, is not followed by any definite alternative conclusions or innovating perspectives. The authors merely hope that, in the human society of the future, "human diversities" will not be criminalized by the establishment in power.

It is therefore necessary to go deeper into these problems so as to develop a third stage in the establishment of a "new criminology", which overrides all forms of determinism, is grounded upon the respect of the dignity and autonomy of man, considered as the synthesis of a complex individual and social reality.

Criminology studies antisocial behavior for the purpose of establishing its motives (fundamental research) and working out suitable prevention and treatment programs (applied research).

The concept of "antisocial behavior" is based upon two principles:

— personality, where behavior originates, which concerns the individual, considered not only as a biological organism but also as the bearer of cultural values and member of a social group;

— antisociality, ranging from simple maladjustment to more defined forms of antisociality and finally to criminal behavior (antisociality as a crime).

These problems must first be considered in a positive sense. To this end it may be useful to carry out, from a theoretical viewpoint, a preliminary examination of the general concept of "value," which may be considered either in a relative or absolute sense: a contrast overcome by the theories which define value not only as a "possibility of making a choice" but also as an "intelligent discipline" of the choices. The theory of values is inclined to determine the "authentic" possibilities of choosing.

It is obvious how a discussion of these arguments, which have already been made the subject-matter of profound analyses in the philosophical field, may become the necessary

9

premise for a criminology which intends to qualify as a science.

"Crime prevention and treatment programs" are also based on two general "principles":

— socialization, the learning process which favors the development and maturity of the personality, whereby the individual becomes an acknowledged and cooperative member of a social group, thus achieving an adaptation of his behavior to the rules of the group;

— re-education, the learning process which favors the resocialization of the individual who had previously behaved in an antisocial manner, opposed to the rules of the social group to which he belongs.

The principle of socialization is the basis of the prevention activity while the principle of re-education is the basis of the delinquency treatment activity (be it merely punitive or therapeutical and rehabilitative). Thus, the requirement which gives prevention priority over treatment, leads to the need of strengthening the principle of socialization as against the principle of re-education.

These aspects of criminology must now be considered from a viewpoint that differs from the traditional one, i.e. in a "positive" sense, which means that all "re-educational" activity must be considered as a function of the principle of socialization, meant to be the natural process of approach to and communication with the other members of the group to which the individual belongs. It ensues that all these members must also be suitably prepared to contribute toward the re-educational and, above all, socialization activity.

Should this preparation be lacking, even the extra-mural treatment measures, as an alternative to imprisonment, would be to no avail. This problem acquires an even wider meaning when the present tendency of entrusting the citizens' "community" with prevention and treatment tasks is taken into account. Positive initiatives in this field have already been reported.

It is therefore important that the meaning of our own responsibilities be made clear. This is a matter of "responsible citizenship" which involves all the members of a community. Consequently there arises the need of establishing how the family, the schools, the magistracy, the Church, society and the criminal justice system may contribute toward the development of a real civic awareness both in the general public and in the individual whose behavior has already deviated into criminality.

A new critical approach in criminology may now be outlined, an interdisciplinary approach based upon the study of the development of values in the field of fundamental research, and of responsible citizenship in the field of applied research, for the purpose of prevention and treatment.

In order for criminology to evolve in this direction, two kinds of action should be taken:

1) in respect to the experts of the fundamental disciplines, an effort to obtain and make contributions that will clarify the meaning and implications of certain concepts in the field of values, particular-

ly those pertaining to the principle of personality, sociality, legality, and responsible citizenship; and,

2) in respect to the experts operating in the practical field an effort to elaborate, in a positive sense certain problems of present-day criminology, such as prevention and treatment problems, in the light of the socialization and re-education principle.

With due consideration to the above mentioned perspectives, and under the sponsorship of the Aquinas Fund, the International Society for Criminology presents the "Aquinas Fund International Lectures on Responsible Citizenship." This year's lecture is the first of a series of lectures that will be held every two years. Michael Novak has prepared a paper on this subject. I thank him very much for accepting our invitation.

Professor Albert Reiss, Jr., will comment on Mr. Novak's paper.

The society plans further studies and researches on the present problems of criminology, viewed in a perspective centered upon man, whose purpose is to favor the development of man's autonomy, in full respect of his dignity.

*Director, Institute of Legal Medicine, International Center for Clinical Criminology, Genoa University; President, International Society for Criminology.

Introduction: The Rediscovery of Character*
by James Q. Wilson

The most important change in how one defines the public interest that I have witnessed — and experienced — over the last twenty years has been a deepening concern for the development of character in the citizenry. An obvious indication of this shift has been the rise of such social issues as abortion and school prayer. A less obvious but I think more important change has been the growing awareness that a variety of public problems can only be understood — and perhaps addressed — if they are seen as arising out of a defect in character formation.

The Public Interest began publication at about the time that economics was becoming the preferred mode of policy analysis. Its very first issue in 1965 contained an article by Daniel Patrick Moynihan hailing the triumph of macroeconomics: "Men are learning how to make an industrial economy work" as evidenced by the impressive ability of economists not only to predict economic events accurately but to control them by, for example, delivering on the promise of full employment. Six months later I published an essay suggesting that poverty be dealt with by direct income

*Reprinted from THE PUBLIC INTEREST, 81 (Fall 1985), pp. 3-16.

transfers in the form of a negative income tax or family allowances. In the next issue, James Tobin made a full-scale proposal for a negative income tax and Virginia Held welcomed program planning and budgeting to Washington as a means for rationalizing the allocative decisions of government, a topic enlarged upon the following year by a leading practitioner of applied economics, William Gorham. Meanwhile, Thomas C. Schelling had published a brilliant economic analysis of organized crime and Christopher Jencks a call for a voucher system that would allow parents to choose among public and private purveyors of education. In a later issue, Gordon Tullock explained the rise in crime as a consequence of individuals responding rationally to an increase in the net benefit of criminality.

There were criticisms of some of these views. Alvin L. Schorr, James C. Vadakian, and Nathan Glazer published essays in 1966, 1968, and 1969 attacking aspects of the negative income tax, and Aaron Wildavsky expressed his skepticism about program budgeting. But the criticisms themselves often accepted the economic assumptions of those being criticized. Schorr, for example, argued that the negative income tax was unworkable because it did not resolve the conflict between having a strong work incentive (and thus too small a payment to many needy individuals) and providing an adequate payment to the needy (and thus weakening the work incentive and making the total cost politically unacceptable). Schorr proposed instead a system of children's allowances and improved social security coverage, but he did not dissent from the view that the only thing wrong with poor people was that they did not have enough money and the conviction that they had a "right" to enough. Tobin was quick to point out that he and Schorr were on the same side, differing only in minor details.

A central assumption of economics is that "tastes" (which include what non-economists would call values and beliefs, as well as interests) can be taken as given and are not problematic. All that is interesting in human behavior is how it changes in response to changes in the costs and benefits of alternative courses of action. All that is necessary in public policy is to arrange the incentives confronting voters, citizens, firms, bureaucrats, and politicians so that they will behave in a socially optimal way. An optimal policy involves an efficient allocation — one that purchases the greatest amount of some good for a given cost, or minimizes the cost of a given amount of some good.

This view so accords with common sense in countless aspects of ordinary life that, for many purposes, its value is beyond dispute. Moreover, enough political decisions are manifestly so inefficient or rely so excessively on issuing commands (instead of arranging incentives) that very little harm and much good can be done by urging public officials to "think economically" about public policy. But over the last two decades, this nation has come face to face with problems that do not seem to respond, or respond enough, to changes in incentives. They do not respond, it seems, because the people whose behavior we wish to change do not have the right "tastes" or discount the future too heavily. To put it plainly, they lack character. Consider four areas of public policy: schooling, welfare, public finance, and crime.

SCHOOLING

Nothing better illustrates the changes in how we think about policy than the problem of finding ways to improve educational attainment and student conduct in the schools. One of the first reports of the 1966 study on education by James Coleman and his associates appeared in this magazine. As every expert on schooling knows, that massive survey of public schools found that differences in the objective inputs to such schools — pupil-teacher ratios, the number of books in the library, per pupil expenditures, the age and quality of buildings — had no independent effect on student achievement as measured by standardized tests of verbal ability.

But as many scholars have forgotten, the Coleman Report also found that educational achievement was profoundly affected by the family background and peer-group environment of the pupil. And those who did notice this finding understandably despaired of devising a program that would improve the child's family background or social environment. Soon, many specialists had concluded that schools could make no difference in a child's life prospects, and so the burden of enhancing those prospects would have to fall on other measures. (To Christopher Jencks, the inability of the schools to reduce social inequality was an argument for socialism.)

Parents, of course, acted as if the Coleman Report had never been written. They sought, often at great expense, communities that had good schools, never doubting for a moment that they could tell the difference between good ones and bad ones or that this difference in school quality would make a difference in their child's education. The search for good schools in the face of evidence that there was no objective basis for that search seems paradoxical, even irrational.

In 1979, however, Michael Rutter and his colleagues in England published a study that provided support for parental understanding by building on the neglected insights of the Coleman Report. In *Fifteen Thousand Hours*, the Rutter group reported what they learned from following a large number of children from a working class section of inner London as they moved through a dozen non-selective schools in their community. Like Coleman before him, Rutter found that the objective features of the schools made little difference; like almost every other scholar, he found that differences in verbal intelligence at age ten were the best single predictor of educational attainment in the high school years. But unlike Coleman, he looked at differences in that attainment across schools, holding individual ability constant. Rutter found that the schools in inner London had very different effects on their pupils, not only in educational achievement but also in attendance, classroom behavior, and even delinquency. Some schools did a better job than others in teaching children and managing their behavior.

The more effective schools had two distinctive characteristics. First, they had a more balanced mix of children — that is, they contained a substantial number of children of at least average intellectual ability. By contrast, schools that were less effective had a disproportionate number of low-ability students. If you are a pupil of below average ability, you do better, both academically and behaviorally, if you attend a school with a large number of students who are somewhat abler than you. The intellectual abilities of the students, it turned out, were far more important than their ethnic or class characteristics in producing this desirable balance.

Second, the more effective schools had a distinctive ethos: an emphasis on academic achievement, the regular assignment of homework, the consistent and fair use of rewards (especially praise) to enforce generally agreed-upon standards of conduct, and energetic teacher involvement in directing classroom work. Subsequent research by others has generally confirmed the Rutter account, so much so that educational specialists are increasingly discussing what has come to be known as the the "effective schools" model.

What is striking about the desirable school ethos is that it so obviously resembles what almost every developmental psychologist describes as the desirable family ethos. Parents who are warm and caring but who also use discipline in a fair and consistent manner are those parents who, other things being equal, are least likely to produce delinquent offspring. A decent family is one that instills a decent character in its children; a good school is one that takes up and continues in a constructive manner this development of character.

Teaching students with the right mix of abilities and in an atmosphere based on the appropriate classroom ethos may be easier in private than in public schools, a fact which helps explain why Coleman (joined now by Thomas Hoffer and Sally Kilgore) was able to suggest in the 1982 book, *High School Achievement*, that private and parochial high schools may do somewhat better than public ones in improving the vocabulary and mathematical skills of students and that this private-school advantage may be largely the result of the better behavior of children in those classrooms. In the authors' words, "achievement and discipline are intimately intertwined." Public schools that combine academic demands and high disciplinary standards produce greater educational achievement than public schools that do not. As it turns out, private and parochial schools are better able to sustain these desirable habits of work behavior — this greater display of good character — than are public ones.

INTRODUCTION

WELFARE

Besides the Coleman Report, another famous document appeared at about the time *The Public Interest* was launched — the Moynihan Report on the problems of the black family (officially, the U.S. Department of Labor document entitled *The Negro Family: The Case for National Action*). The storm of controversy that report elicited is well-known. Despite Moynihan's efforts to keep the issue alive by publishing in these pages several essays on the welfare problem in America, the entire subject of single-parent families in particular and black families in general became an occasion for the exchange of mutual recriminations instead of a topic of scientific inquiry and policy entrepreneurship. Serious scholarly work, if it existed at all, was driven underground, and policymakers were at pains to avoid the matter except, occasionally, under the guise of "welfare reform" which meant (if you were a liberal) raising the level of benefits or (if you were a conservative) cutting them. By the end of the 1960s, almost everybody in Washington had in this sense become a conservative; welfare reform, as Moynihan remarked, was dead.

Twenty years after the Moynihan Report, Moynihan himself could deliver at Harvard a lecture in which he repeated the observations he had made in 1965, but this time to an enthusiastic audience and widespread praise in the liberal media. At the same time, Glenn C. Loury, a black economist, could publish in these pages an essay in which he observed that almost everything Moynihan had said in 1965 had proved true except in one sense — today, single-parent families are twice as common as they were when Moynihan first called the matter to public attention. The very title of Loury's essay suggested how times had changed: Whereas leaders once spoke of "welfare reform" as if it were a problem of finding the most cost-effective way to distribute aid to needy families, Loury was now prepared to speak of it as "The Moral Quandary of the Black Community."

Two decades that could have been devoted to thought and experimentation had been frittered away. We are no closer today than we were in 1965 to understanding why black children are usually raised by one parent rather than by two or exactly what consequences, beyond the obvious fact that such families are very likely to be poor, follows from this pattern of family life. To the extent the matter was addressed at all, it was usually done by assuming that welfare payments provided an incentive for families to dissolve. To deal with this, some people embraced the negative income tax (or as President Nixon rechristened it, the Family Assistance Plan) because it would provide benefits to all poor families, broken or not, and thus remove incentive for dissolution.

There were good reasons to be somewhat skeptical of that view. If the system of payments under the program for Aid to Families of Dependent Children (AFDC) was to blame for the rise in single-parent families, why did the rise occur so dramatically among blacks but not to nearly the same extent among whites? If AFDC provided an incentive for men to beget children without assuming responsibility for supporting them, why was the illegitimacy rate rising even in states that did not require the father to be absent from the home for the family to obtain assistance? If AFDC created so perverse a set of incentives, why did these incentives have so large an effect in the 1960s and 1970s (when single-parent families were increasing by leaps and bounds) and so little, if any, such effect in the 1940s and 1950s (when such families scarcely increased at all)? And if AFDC were the culprit, how is it that poor, single-parent families rose in number during a decade (the 1970s) when the value of AFDC benefits in real dollars was declining?

Behavior does change with changes in incentives. The results of the negative income tax experiments certainly show that. In the Seattle and Denver experiments, the rate of family dissolution was much higher among families who received the guaranteed annual income than among similar families who did not — 36 percent higher in the case of whites, 42 percent higher in the case of blacks. Men getting the cash benefits reduced their hours of work by 9 percent, women by 20 percent, and young males without families by 43 percent.

Charles Murray, whose 1984 book, *Losing Ground*, has done so much to focus attention on the problem of welfare, generally endorses the economic explanation for the decline of two-parent families. The evidence from the negative income tax experiments is certainly consistent with his view, and he makes a good case that the liberalization of welfare eligibility rules in the 1960s contributed to the sudden increase in the AFDC caseload. But as he is the first to admit, the data do not exist to offer a fully tested explanation of the rise of single-parent families; the best he can do is to offer a mental experiment showing how young, poor men and women might rationally respond to the alternative benefits of work for a two-parent family and welfare payments for a one-parent one. He rejects the notions that character, the *Zeitgeist*, or cultural differences are necessary to an explanation. But he cannot show that young, poor men and women in fact responded to AFDC as he assumes they did, nor can he explain the racial differences in rates or the rise in caseloads at a time of declining benefits. He notes an alternative explanation that cannot be ruled out: During the 1960s, a large number of persons who once thought of being on welfare as a temporary and rather embarrassing expedient came to regard it as a right that they would not be deterred from exercising. The result of that change can be measured: Whereas in 1967, 63 percent of the persons eligible for AFDC were on the rolls, by 1970 91 percent were.

In short, the character of a significant number of persons changed. To the extent one thinks that change was fundamentally wrong, then, as Loury has put it, the change creates a moral problem. What does one do about such a moral problem? Lawrence Mead has suggested invigorating the work requirement associated with welfare, so that anyone exercising a "right" to welfare will come to understand that there is a corresponding obligation. Murray has proposed altering the incentives by increasing the difficulty of getting welfare or the shame of having it or so as to provide positive rewards for not having children, at least out of wedlock. But nobody has yet come to grips with how one might test a way of using either obligations or incentives to alter character so that people who once thought it good to sire or bear illegitimate children will now think it wrong.

PUBLIC FINANCE

We have a vast and rising governmental deficit. Amidst the debate about how one might best reduce that deficit (or more typically, reduce the rate of increase in it), scarcely anyone asks why we have not always had huge deficits.

If you believe that voters and politicians seek rationally to maximize their self-interest, then it would certainly be in the interest of most people to transfer wealth from future generations to present ones. If you want the federal government to provide you with some benefit and you cannot persuade other voters to pay for your benefit with higher taxes, then you should be willing to have the government borrow to pay for that benefit. Since every voter has something he would like from the government, each has an incentive to obtain that

benefit with funds to be repaid by future generations. There are, of course, some constraints on
unlimited debt financing. Accumulated debt
charges from past generations must be financed by
this generation, and if these charges are heavy there
may well develop some apprehension about adding
to them. If some units of government default on
their loans, there are immediate economic consequences. But these constraints are not strong
enough to inhibit more than marginally the rational
desire to let one's grandchildren pay (in inflation-
devalued dollars) the cost of present indulgences.

That being so, why is it that large deficits, except
in wartime, have been a feature of public finance
only in the past few decades? What kept voters and
politicians from buying on credit heavily and con-
tinuously beginning with the first days of the
republic?

James M. Buchanan, in his 1984 presidential address to the Western Economic Association, has offered one explanation for this paradox. He has suggested that public finance was once subject to a
moral constraint — namely, that it was right to pay
as you go and accumulate capital and wrong to borrow heavily and squander capital. Max Weber, of
course, had earlier argued that essential to the rise
of capitalism was a widely shared belief (he ascrib-
ed it to Protestantism) in the moral propriety of
deferring present consumption for future benefits.
Buchanan has recast this somewhat: He argues that
a Victorian morality inhibited Anglo-American
democracies from giving in to their selfish desire to

25

beggar their children.

Viewed in this way, John Maynard Keynes was not simply an important economist, he was a moral revolutionary. He subjected to rational analysis the conventional restraints on deficit financing, not in order to show that debt was always good but to prove that it was not necessarily bad. Deficit financing should be judged, he argued, by its practical effect, not by its moral quality.

Buchanan is a free-market economist, and thus a member of a group not ordinarily given to explaining behavior in any terms other than the pursuit of self-interest narrowly defined. This fact makes all the more significant his argument that economic analysts must understand "how morals impact on choice, and especially how an erosion of moral precepts can modify the established functioning of economic and political institutions."

A rejoinder can be made to the Buchanan explanation of deficit financing. Much of the accumulated debt is a legacy of having fought wars, a legacy that can be justified on both rational and moral grounds (who wishes to lose a war, or to leave for one's children a Europe dominated by Hitler?). Another part of the debt exists because leaders miscalculated the true costs of desirable programs. According to projections made in 1965, Medicare was supposed to cost less than $9 billion a year in 1990; in 1985, the bill was already running in excess of $70 billion a year. Military pensions seemed the right thing to do when men were being called to service, only in retrospect is their total cost appreciated. The Reagan tax cuts were not designed to impose heavy debts on our children but to stimulate investment and economic growth; only later did it become obvious that they have contributed far more to the deficit than to economic growth. The various subsidies given to special interest groups for long seemed like a small price to pay for insuring the support of a heterogeneous people for a distant government, no one could have foreseen their cumulative burden.

No doubt there is some truth in the proposition that our current level of debt is the result of miscalculation and good intentions gone awry. But what strengthens Buchanan's argument, I believe, is the direction of these miscalculations (if that is what they were) and the nature of these good intentions. In almost every instance, leaders proposing a new policy erred in the direction of understating rather than overstating future costs; in almost every instance, evidence of a good intention was taken to be government action rather than inaction. Whether one wishes to call it a shift in moral values or not, one must be struck by the systematic and consistent bias in how we debated public programs beginning in the 1930s but especially in the 1960s. It is hard to remember it now, but there once was a time, lasting from 1789 to well into the 1950s, when the debate over almost any new proposal was about whether it was *legitimate* for the government to do this at all. Those were certainly the terms in which Social Security, civil rights, Medicare, and government regulation of business were first addressed. By the 1960s, the debate was much different; how much should we spend (not, should we spend anything at all); how can a policy be made cost-effective (not, should we have such a policy in the first place). The character of public discourse changed and, I suspect, in ways that suggest a change in the nature of public character.

I have written more about crime than any other policy issue, and so my remarks on our changing understanding of this problem are to a large degree remarks about changes in my own way of thinking about it. On no subject have the methods of economics and policy analysis had greater or more salutary effect than on scholary discussions of criminal justice. For purposes of designing public policies, it has proved useful to think of would-be offenders as mostly young males who compare the net benefits of crime with those of work and leisure. Such thinking, and the rather considerable body of evidence that supports it, leads us to expect that changes in the net benefits of crime affect the level of crime in society. To the extent that policymakers and criminologists have become less hostile to the idea of altering behavior by altering its consequences, progress has been made. Even if the amount by which crime is reduced by these measures is modest (as I think in a free society it will be), the pursuit of these policies conforms more fully than does the rehabilitative idea to our concept of justice — namely, that each person should receive his due.

But long-term changes in crime rates exceed

anything that can be explained by either rational calculation or the varying proportion of young males in the population. Very little in either contemporary economics or conventional criminology equips us to understand the decline in reported crime rates during the second half of the nineteenth century and the first part of the twentieth despite rapid industrialization and urbanization, a large influx of poor immigrants, the growing ethnic heterogeneity of society, and widening class cleavages. Very little in the customary language of policy analysis helps us explain why Japan should have such abnormally low crime rates despite high population densities, a history that glorifies samurai violence, a rather permissive pattern of child-rearing, the absence of deep religious convictions, and the remarkably low ratio of police officers to citizens.

In an essay in this magazine in 1983 I attempted to explain the counter-intuitive decline in crime during the period after the Civil War in much the same terms that David H. Bayley had used in a 1976 article dealing with crime in Japan. In both cases, distinctive cultural forces helped restrain individual self-expression. In Japan, these forces subject an individual to the informal social controls of family and neighbors by making him extremely sensitive to the good opinion of others. The controls are of long standing and have so far remained largely intact despite the individualizing tendencies of modernization. In the United States, by contrast, these cultural forces have operated only in certain periods, and when they were effective it was as a result of a herculean effort by scores of voluntary associations specially created for the purpose.

In this country as well as in England, a variety of enterprises — Sunday schools, public schools, temperance movements, religious revivals, YMCAs, the Children's Aid Society — were launched in the first half of the nineteenth century that had in common the goal of instilling a "self-activating, self-regulating, all-purpose inner control." The objects of these efforts were those young men who, freed from the restraints of family life on the farms, had moved to the boardinghouses of the cities in search of economic opportunities. We lack any reliable measure of the effect of these efforts, save one — the extraordinary reduction in the per capita consumption of alcoholic beverages that occurred between 1830 (when the temperance efforts began in eanest) and 1850 and that persisted (despite an upturn during and just after Civil Way) for the rest of the century.

We now refer to this period as one in which "Victorian morality" took hold; the term itself, at least as now employed, reflects the condescension in which that ethos has come to be regarded. Modernity, as I have argued elsewhere, involves, at least in elite opinion, replacing the ethic of self-control with that of self-expression. Some great benefits have flowed from this change, including the liberation of youthful energies to pursue new ideas in art, music, literature, politics, and economic enterprise. But the costs are just as real, at least for those young persons who have not already acquired a decent degree of self-restraint and other-regardingness.

The view that crime has social and cultural as well as economic causes is scarcely new. Hardly any lay person, and only a few scholars, would deny that family and neighborhood affect individual differences in criminality. But what of it? How, as I asked in 1974, might a government remake bad families into good ones, especially if it must be done on a large scale? How might the government of a free society reshape the core values of its people and still leave them free?

They were good questions then and they remain good ones today. In 1974 there was virtually no reliable evidence that any program seeking to prevent crime by changing attitudes and values had succeeded for any large number of persons. In 1974 I could only urge policymakers to postpone the effort to eliminate the root causes of crime in favor of using those available policy instruments — target hardening, job training, police deployment, court sentences — that might have a marginal effect at a reasonable cost on the commission of crime. Given what we knew then and know now, acting as if crime is the result of individuals freely choosing among competing alternatives may be the best we can do.

In retrospect, nothing I have written about crime so dismayed some criminologists as this preference for doing what is possible rather than attempting what one wishes were possible. My purpose was to substitute the experimental method for personal ideology; this effort has led some people to suspect I was really trying to substitute my ideology for theirs. Though we all have beliefs that color our views, I would hope that everybody would try to keep that coloration under control by constant reference to the test of practical effect. What works?

With time and experience we have learned a bit more about what works. There are now some glimmers of hope that certain experimental projects aimed at preparing children for school and equipping parents to cope with unruly offspring may reduce the rate at which these youngsters later commit delinquent acts. Richard J. Herrnstein and I have written about these and related matters in *Crime and Human Nature*. Whether further tests and repeated experiments will confirm that these glimmers emanate from the mother lode of truth and not from fool's gold, no one can yet say. But we know how to find out. If we discover that these ideas can be made to work on a large scale (and not just in the hands of a few gifted practitioners), then we will be able to reduce crime by, in effect, improving character.

CHARACTER AND POLICY

The traditional understanding of politics was that its goal was to improve the character of its citizens. The American republic was, as we know, founded on a very different understanding — that of taking human nature pretty much as it was and hoping that personal liberty could survive political action if ambition were made to counteract ambition. The distinctive nature of the American system has led many of its supporters (to say nothing of its critics) to argue that it should be indifferent to character formation. Friend and foe alike are fond of applying to government Samuel Goldwyn's response to the person who asked what message was to be found in his films: If you want to send a message, use Western Union.

Since I yield to no one in my admiration for what the Founders created, I do not wish to argue the fundamental proposition. But the federal government today is very different from what it was in 1787, 1887, or even 1957. If we wish it to address the problems of family disruption, welfare dependency, crime in the streets, educational inadequacy, or even public finance properly understood, then government, by the mere fact that it defines these states of affairs as problems, acknowledges that human character is, in some degree, defective and that it intends to alter it. The local governments of village and township always understood this, of course, because they always had responsibility for shaping character. The public school movement, for example, was from the beginning chiefly aimed at moral instruction. The national government could afford to manage its affairs by letting ambition counteract ambition because what was originally at stake in national affairs — creating and maintaining a reasonably secure commercial regime — lent itself naturally to the minimal attentions of a limited government operated and restrained by the reciprocal force of mutual self-interest.

It is easier to acknowledge the necessary involvement of government in character formation than it is to prescribe how this responsibility should be carried out. The essential first step is to acknowledge that at root, in almost every area of important public concern, we are seeking to induce persons to act virtuously, whether as schoolchildren, applicants for public assistance, would-be lawbreakers, or voters and public officials. Not only is such conduct desirable in its own right, it appears now to be necessary if large improvements are to be made in those matters we consider problems: schooling, welfare, crime, and public finance.

By virtue, I mean habits of moderate action; more specifically, acting with due restraint on one's impulses, due regard for the rights of others, and reasonable concern for distant consequences. Scarcely anyone favors bad character or a lack of virtue, but it is all too easy to deride a policy of improving character by assuming that this implies a nation of moralizers delivering banal homilies to one another.

Virtue is not learned by precept, however; it is learned by the regular repetition of right actions. We are induced to do the right thing with respect to small matters, and in time we persist in doing the right thing because now we have come to take pleasure in it. By acting rightly with respect to small things, we are more likely to act rightly with respect to large ones. If this view sounds familiar, it should; it is Aristotle's. Let me now quote him directly: "We become just by the practice of just actions, self-controlled by exercising self-control."

Seen in this way, there is no conflict between economic thought and moral philosophy: The latter simply supplies a fuller statement of the uses to which the former can and should be put. We want our families and schools to induce habits of right conduct; most parents and teachers do this by arranging the incentives confronting youngsters in the ordinary aspects of their daily lives so that right action routinely occurs.

What economics neglects is the important subjective consequence of acting in accord with a proper array of incentives: people come to feel pleasure in right action and guilt in wrong action. These feelings of pleasure and pain are not mere "tastes" that policy analysts should take as given; they are the central constraints on human avarice and sloth, the very core of a decent character. A course of action cannot be evaluated simply in terms of its cost-effectiveness, because the consequences of following a given course — if it is followed often enough and regularly enough — is to teach those who follow it what society thinks is right and wrong.

Conscience and character, naturally, are not enough. Rules and rewards must still be employed; indeed, given the irresistible appeal of certain courses of action — such as impoverishing future generations for the benefit of the present one — only some rather draconian rules may suffice. But for most social problems that deeply trouble us, the need is to explore, carefully and experimentally, ways of strengthening the formation of character among the very young. In the long run, the public interest depends on private virtue.

CHARACTER AND CRIME
An Inquiry Into The Causes
Of The Virtue Of Nations

Most people most of the time start at the wrong end. Avalanches of books discuss the causes of poverty. That this is a useless inquiry becomes clear the moment one asks oneself what one would have, if one had the answer to the question, "What causes poverty?" One would then know how to make poverty. Wonderful! Quite obviously, the more interesting and fruitful question — which waited until 1776 for its first appearance in intellectual history — is, "What are the causes of wealth?"

That famous question of Adam Smith had a communal purpose.[1] His inquiry did not concern the wealth of *individuals*. The question he asked regarded the whole of human society, of all nations, and of course of each nation one-by-one.

Similarly, the subject assigned me being "crime," I intend to inquire into the problematic rather than the obvious part; *viz.*, *not* "What are the causes of crime?" but, "What are the causes of virtue?" Crime is what you have in the absence of virtue; it is virtue that needs to be explained. And I approach this task with communal purpose, keeping in view the *social* causes of the *social* virtues in *societies* taken as wholes. I wish to write about the culture of virtue, as one significant means for reducing the frequency of crime.

Clearly, I write as a philosopher, not as a social scientist (it was precisely for that approach that, however ill-equipped, I was invited to prepare these modest reflections). That Adam Smith was no economist when he penned *The Wealth of Nations*, only a moral philosopher, affords me some small courage.

1. INTRODUCTION AND DEFINITIONS

Virtue, not always present, juts up out of human history; its appearance is not self-explanatory.

Human beings are prone to heedless self-expression; wanton self-indulgence; the practices of deceit and flattery and exaggeration and outright lie; the impulse to attain whatever they want; the desire to humiliate others and to exhibit cruelty (towards their own spouses and children, for example); powerful feelings of covetousness and lust; passions of anger, rage, and ambition; the urge to master others and to treat them as slaves; and other sundry impulsions toward vice and crime. What is amazing is not that human beings are sometimes criminal. What requires explanation is the fact that all are not. What requires explanation is virtue.

In one's ear, of course, one hears already the rumbling objection: But even among the most criminally prone class, young males between 16 and 25, only about six percent will become involved in serious crime;[2] the others are "normal." It is the *deviant* who must be explained.

Although it is easy to sympathize with it, such an objection does not go deep enough. The sort of *explanation* I am looking for aims at the free, surprising, amazing *existence* of habits of acting well (virtue). I admire generous, creative, dutiful, non-criminal, public-spirited, civic-minded, other-regarding, reasoned and measured behavior. What is so astonishing to me is that virtue exists at all. Why should there be virtue, when there could so easily be vice, crime, and folly? And how does a society see to it that such virtue becomes, so to speak, routine, systematic, highly probable, even "normal"? This is a stupendous achievement. How it is effected deserves to be much more deeply studied.

It is no surprise to me that there are criminals. The human being who has not fought inwardly against criminal impulses deserves to be immortalized. The certain risk run by such a person, if such a person there is, is to be thought by others insufficiently human.

I have so far been using the words "crime," "vice," and "folly" loosely and as if synonymous. Further clarity demands, however, that, henceforth, at least the two words "virtue" and "crime," as used in this essay, should have exact meanings. By *crime*, I shall mean those serious offenses against the law whose statistics are regularly kept by the U.S. Department of Justice (and similar bodies in other countries). I do so in order to keep my meaning as simple and plain as possible. Further, this definition seems to have virtually universal relevance. The serious crimes involved are regarded as such almost everywhere.

By *virtue*, however, my argument requires me to mean two things. The broadest and lowest-level meaning, sufficient for this essay, is the non-commission of crime. Suppose a citizenry to be as mediocre upon the moral scale as you please, allowing only that none of them ever commits a crime: Such a society would be classified, most certainly as this world goes, a virtuous society. It would be so classified even though it were marked by indolence, timidity, and numerous other flaws of character, in themselves quite unattractive when compared to human possibility. A utilitarian philosophy might produce such a society, an entire people living at a low level of self-sacrifice, individually self-expressive and self-indulgent, but taking care never to hurt any other or the commonweal. I would not find such a society completely attractive. Or even fully moral. And I cannot myself believe that it would long remain without crime. But, as a supposition, it would give sufficient content to the word *virtue* for the following argument.

The second meaning goes beyond the barest minimum needed for my argument. In this second meaning, *virtue* means not merely the non-commission of crime. It means, in the Aristotelian sense, that full panoply of human moral skills and settled dispositions that constitutes *character*.[3] It means the classic cardinal virtues: justice, fortitude, temperance, and practical wisdom. It means a compatible mix of all those other virtues identified by religious traditions, literary stories, the sages, and persons of common sense down through history: patience, kindness, cooperativeness, loyalty, initiative, self-reliance, magnanimity, frugality, and the like. No one has all the virtues; everyone has some weaknesses. Thus, persons of much-admired character may differ considerably from one another except in this: all fall short of perfection. Character, constituted by a whole range of virtuous dispositions, is as various as personal artistry can make it.

In brief, virtues are inborn or learned tendencies that make their corresponding actions occur spontaneously, easily, and without effort. It must be stressed again that in no one are *all* human virtues inborn. Most human beings must acquire most of the virtues by persistent, painstaking, and constant effort. The struggle to acquire virtues — to add to one's repertory thereof — normally takes a lifetime. All of us often fall short. For this reason, forgiveness for the faults of others and equanimity regarding our own persistent failings (combined with the resolve to do better) are themselves highly regarded human virtues; the name given them, "tolerance," is a noble one. *Errare humanum est.* "To err is human; to forgive, divine."

In the worldly polity, Aristotle wrote, in trying to teach virtue and to reduce vice, we must be satisfied with "a tincture of virtue."[4] Wisdom consists in not expecting too much of human material. This is true, even though ethics consists in aspiring toward the ever fuller development of a full complement of virtues: i.e., toward human perfection in action. For Aristotle, each man and each woman must fashion himself or herself in the full range of human skills, with all the care of a sculptor sculpting a perfect statue: not, however, in order to be pleasing to look at (as in complacent conscience) but in order to act well.[5] Acting well in all circumstances, even when surprised or under pressure, is the highest form of ordinary human happiness.[6] (The highest extraordinary form of human happiness is to be one with God in silent contemplation.)[7]

This second, higher sense of human virtue, I believe, is in practice necessary to my argument. Whereas the first, lower level of virtue — the non-commission of crime — technically meets the requirements of the argument, only the constant effort of a society to form its members in the second sense is likely in practice to produce the good society. To attain the lower level of virtue would be quite an achievement for any society. Yet it does seem to be a valid rule of the moral life that a man's reach must exceed his grasp. Even when a society aims at the highest virtue, it is virtually certain to fall short. Criminal acts occur in all known societies. So many and so great are the impulses toward criminal behavior, and so many are the surprising and temptation-laden contingencies of every human life, that even citizens of high virtue sometimes fall. When many citizens are content with the lower levels of virtue, the probabilities that higher numbers of them will fall occasionally into crime are bound to jump.

My thesis, then, is that *criminal behavior follows from a defect of virtue. Persistent criminal behavior follows from serious flaws in character.*

The criminal is a mal-formed or ill-developed human person. These points may be put another way. Crime does not just "happen." It would occur far more frequently if human beings did not choose to resist criminal behavior. *As human persons are responsible for their own character, so they are responsible for their criminal acts. Crime is chosen.*[8] *It is, for some, a chosen way of life.* Criminal action is always, in all times and in all places, an option for every human being. What is amazing is its relative infrequency.

A further distinction is necessary. Criminal acts act against *virtue*, but they are simultaneously acts against duly constituted *law*. It is necessary to say this to distinguish crimes from vices, i.e., from acts against virtue that are *not* simultaneously forbidden in law. There are not only private vices such as, e.g., overeating, but also social vices, such as calumniating or slandering other persons in the company of others. While for the purposes of this essay I am defining *virtue* as over against *crime*, it is important to note that *crime* indicates only a small portion of the field of *vice*.

The subject of this lecture, then, is how to effectuate the relative infrequency of crime. Put more positively, it is an inquiry into the causes of virtue — particularly, the *cultural* causes of virtue.

2. CRIME AND THE GREAT TRADITION

There is a late-Calvinist quip of which I must here avail myself: "The fellow who said man is totally depraved couldn't have been all bad." The point of view of my introductory remarks is implicit in that quip. This point of view is to be found in Aristotle, in St. Thomas Aquinas, in *The Federalist* — and in many other treasures of the ages. While such citations do not argue that this point of view is universal, they do save it from being provincial and merely contemporary. One can find it, to mention only a few examples, in Athens three centuries before Christ; in Italy and Paris some fifteen centuries later, during the lifetime of Aquinas (1225-1274); and in the Whig tradition of Britain, France and America some six to seven centuries after Aquinas (in Madison, Jefferson, Tocqueville, Burke, Acton, etc.) William James, in trying to express a distinctively American ethic, sought eagerly to link it to this earlier long tradition.[9]

There is no good name for this tradition, although it has been called "the perennial philosophy," "the public philosophy," and (by F. A. Hayek[10]) "the Whig tradition." While it has a long tradition, it cannot properly be thought of as "conservative," because it is committed to concepts of responsibility, reason, human development, and progress. It cannot be called "individualistic," because since at least the time of Aristotle it has recognized the role of politics, culture, and community in the work of moral development. While consistent with the teachings

45

of Judaism and Christianity, it has been expressed in secular terms by nonbelievers, agnostics, and atheists, since its appeal is to human dignity, personal accountability, and common sense. I refer to it as the Great Tradition, since its dynamic lies embedded in Western legal structures (analogously also in other cultures) and in great moral classics for three thousand years.

The point of view of the Great Tradition conveys two distinct affirmations. First, every human being sometimes sins; that is, does evil and is capable of criminal action. Second, most human beings most of the time are creative, generous, good — in a word, virtuous. This double affirmation asserts that human beings, while not totally depraved, carry within them the power of evil deeds, on the one hand; and, on the other hand, that virtue, while not to be universally expected in human action, is quite natural to human beings. These are quite sensible — and quite staggering — affirmations. For their hidden meaning is that societies can be shaped either to increase or to decrease the probable frequencies of virtue and of crime. As each human being is responsible for his own character, so all collectively are responsible for the institutions under which they choose to live. Culture matters. Institutions matter. A national *ethos* matters.

Since virtue is natural to human beings it is no coercion so to arrange the institutions of culture as to help citizens freely to attain the high degree of virtue of which they are capable. On the other hand, since criminal choices are not only open to human beings, but to be expected in some order of frequency, a lack of social attention to the cultural reinforcement of virtue is likely to result in higher frequencies of crime.

To make this point of view clear, it is useful to distinguish it, briefly, from two contemporary alternatives. Social scientists today seem far more frequently to discuss crime than do philosophers and theologians, and the social sciences are, peculiarly, creatures of the modern era. They are far more likely to accept their point of view from modern, rather than from ancient or medieval, philosophers. That is neither bad nor good in itself, but it does suggest a certain limited horizon.

In particular, two modern traditions seem to lie with special prominence behind contemporary social science with respect to crime: the tradition of Hobbes, which regards crime from the point of view of the individual, and the tradition of Rousseau, which regards crime from the communal point of view of some new alternative society.[11]

The Hobbesian tradition stresses the rationality and will of the individual. It is, in some ways, a pessimistic tradition, expecting from each human being an ineradicable selfishness as regards wealth and ambition, checked solely by fears of violent death and/or related social punishment. Fearful of each other's violence, rational individuals form a state by compact, policing one another thereby, while allowing to each the liberty to pursue self-interest (broadly defined) so long as each does no harm to others. This Hobbesian view does not ask virtue of human beings. Rather, it merely regulates ineradicable self-interest by imposing through institutions a set of costs and benefits that guide the rationality of self-interested individuals in ways that do least harm to others. This is the root of the utilitarian calculus: Raise costs, deter certain behaviors; raise incentives, increase the frequency of other behaviors.

There is a rough plausibility to this view. Its emphasis upon rationality and will save it from treating human beings solely as barbarians and savages. This bestows upon it just sufficient nobility to make it seem reasonable to many. Nonetheless, by treating the individual as empty of virtue — by making virtue seem impossible or, in any case, beside the point — this point of view seriously diminishes human beings. The habit of social analysis it engenders is impersonal. It treats human beings as if they were pigeons scheduled for Skinnerean reinforcement. It encourages the practitioners of its theory to think like statists, as if their task were to "manage" behavior through institutionally imposed costs and benefits, while ignoring the entire middle range of human motivations: faith in God, love of family, pride in heritage, fellow-feeling, delight in good expertly done, etc. It neglects the nourishment of the common fund of ordinary virtue. Since every common act of generosity, fellow-feeling, and altruism escapes its notice, its analytic nets are far too gross.

When Hobbesianism passes over into utilitarianism, it treats individual rationality and

will as simple reflexes, to be manipulated by plan-
ners from above. No doubt, the reflexes upon
which it concentrates its controls are powerful.
Thence the theory's permanent validity. Its radical
flaw, however, is that it neglects those virtues of intellect and will that tremendously complicate
human choice. Because each human being
possesses rationality and will, each person chooses
to differentiate himself or herself from all others by
the character each chooses to resist or to nourish,
to tame or to acquire. Overlooking character and
virtue, Hobbes and his followers diminish human
reality. Reality, as always, takes it revenge.

The second view, which springs generically from
Rousseau, holds that each human being is naturally
virtuous and then corrupted by society. Rousseau
has the advantage of concentrating upon the communal nature of virtue; for him, the task is to create
a new society worthy of man's innate innocence.
Virtue is natural and needs no explanation, and
crime is to be explained as the corruption sown by
evil social structures. Virtue lies in liberating the innocent self. It is society — and its Hobbesian costs
and benefits — that must be overthrown. The flaw
in Rousseau lies in misreading what lies in human
beings in their "raw" state. Anyone who expects
primitive innocence reaps barbarism.

The Aristotelian-Thomistic horizon sketched
earlier is quite different from the horizon of Hobbes
and of Rousseau. Yet it embraces elements from
each. With Hobbes, it attends to the individual, to
rationality, and to will, although the content it

gives each of those three terms is quite different. With Rousseau, it affirms the importance of a communal perspective and the crucial role of social institutions in the nourishment of virtue. Not so manipulative as Hobbes, nor so starry-eyed as Rousseau about some "new" utopian civil society, it sees in human beings immense spiritual resources for good or ill. Wherever they begin, human beings can with sober effort acquire more noble personal capacities and tendencies, as befits their open and developing nature; and they can also fashion for themselves institutions that better nourish the learning of human virtue.

At its founding, the infant United States may have been the most Aristotelian/Thomistic of all nations in its implicit constitution, its way of thinking, and its way of acting. Its founders recognized the evil, ambition, and mischief to which every human heart is prey. They recognized, as well, the virtue to which committed and attentive communities of free men and women could give rise. In establishing a national government — an awesome undertaking for a mere four millions of inhabitants spread up and down a seaboard of some thousand miles of virtually empty country-side — it took care not to create Hobbesian anarchy, on the one hand, or Rousseauean majoritarianism, on the other. Faulted the Founding may be. No matter. The Catholic bishops of the United States meeting in the First Plenary Council of Baltimore in 1884, fully aware of the Catholic traditions of which they were heir, could prudently write: "We consider the establishment of our country's independence, the shaping of its liberties and laws as a special work of Providence, its framers 'building wiser than they knew,' the Almighty's hand guiding them.''[12]

George Will has recently written in his Godkin lectures that this nation was ''ill-founded.''[13]In his view, the Founders paid too little attention to virtue. They designed the Constitution on too secular, too mechanical, too procedural a basis. In the eyes of Will, ''Statecraft is soulcraft.'' The government that abdicates concern for the virtue of its citizens will soon find that, without virtue, the liberties it seeks to defend will have been corrupted. What gives Will's thesis plausibility is the widely shared sense that, by 1983, the virtues of the people *had* been corrupted. The flaw in his thesis is to have turned to government — to ''statecraft'' — as the means to arrest that corruption. (I leave aside the point of fact, on which I am in sharp disagreement with Will, about an alleged deterioration in virtue.)[14]Within limits, of course, political leaders can and must look to the effect of the institutions within their jurisdiction upon the practice of virtue. A mandatory ''virtue-impact'' statement concerning alternative governmental policies would not be entirely out of order; the *human* environment is also an ecological environment. But there are limits. Statecraft ought to be concerned about the *pre-conditions* of ''soulcraft.'' Beyond that, grave danger lurks in political jurisdiction over virtue. In a genuinely pluralistic society, politicians ought not to be responsible for ''soulcraft.''

In this respect, I believe that a society of the American type is not ill-founded, but well-founded, in reserving to free citizens all responsibilities, except those specifically granted to the federal government. Primary responsibilities for "soulcraft" belong to citizens directly, not to government. At the heart of a genuinely pluralistic society, rooted in a conception of free personal conscience and free right of association, there ought to be a "shrine." But that "shrine" should be empty.[15] The shrine signifies that our rights are inalienable, endowed in each of us by a Source well beyond "statecraft." The empty place within that shrine signifies the Transcendence of that Source, which plural peoples in a plural land will name differently.

This does not mean that the public square outside that shrine — to allude to an important book by Richard John Neuhaus, *The Naked Public Square*[16]— ought to be "naked." On the contrary, the public square ought to resonate with argument. Each of the plural communities and unrelated individuals who compose the people ought to make its voice heard. None ought to be timid or shy or intimidated. Each should speak the truth as each sees it, due regard being taken for the requirements of civility. True, not everything that must be said needs to be said *now*. On some matters, it is better to wait; each point has its season. Yet no one should forebear speaking. The point of a *public* square is that each citizen ought to contribute to that civil conversation which is the essential action of a free people. Civilized persons influence one another through reasoned persuasion and in civil conversation. Such conversation is the constitutive act of civilization.[17]

3. CRIME AND CULTURE

Since capacities for virtue and character inhere in human nature and are open to every person, the power of the argument I mean to make applies to every culture. In their magisterial book, *Crime and Human Nature*, James Q. Wilson and Richard J. Herrnstein define some of the universal characteristics of crime across all societies and historical eras, and discuss some of the powerful evidence concerning certain biological roots of crime.[18]While I can pretend to none of their mastery of the evidence afforded by the social sciences, their point of view abuts upon the philosophical (and theological) horizon I mean to explore.

Properly, the point of view of a philosopher concerns the reality of all human persons everywhere. In practice, of course, being embodied and historical creatures like all other humans, philosophers work within limited traditions and conceptual frameworks. This fact makes their work appear to be more provincial than it is — as German philosophy tends to differ from British philosophy, American from Italian, Chinese from French, etc. In *intention*, nonetheless, philosophers are struggling to describe conditions of human existence as these apply to all humans universally. It is in this light that philosophical work is properly judged.

Still, much is to be gained if the philosopher struggles for greater detail and clarity by applying his mind to the materials of one particular culture, while seeking to bring to light those aspects of reality that ought, by analogy, to be true as well in other cultures. Since it is the condition of human beings that, while being one in nature with all others, each is embodied and confined to living within a particular culture, the interplay between such particularity and the universal is complex. A scholar is properly cautious about applying generalizations formed within one culture to other cultures, for he must respect the particularity of each. Still, this is the precise purpose of argument by *analogy*. Such argument proceeds by explicit recognition of the *differences* between the objects compared, while also bringing to light the similarities. Such close work in making distinctions protects the scholar from *equivocation*: that is, from using the same term to express conflicting concrete meanings.

To avoid excessive encumbrance in such detailed comparisons, I have chosen in this essay to confine myself to materials gleaned from the culture of the United States. I leave it to experts in international experiences of character and crime to enunciate more carefully the necessary cross-cultural discernments.

Consider, then, the list of major crimes as enumerated by the Uniform Crime Reporting Program of the U.S. government: Murder and nonnegligent manslaughter; forcible rape; robbery; aggravated assault; burglary; larceny-theft; motor vehicle theft; arson.[19] Universally, these are considered to be crimes. These are not virtuous acts of civil conversation, achieved through reasoned persuasion. These are acts of violence aimed at fulfilling undisciplined desire. Those who desire take. Those who covet seize. Those who intend injury violently inflict it.

How can citizens whose rights in a free society depend upon the same Source as do those whose rights they violently abridge bring themselves to such violence? That is not difficult to answer. Their temptation is known to all. They want to. They desire to. They choose to. To do so is, manifestly, in their power. They do it.

More interesting is why so many do not. More interesting, still, is why history shows us so fluctuating a portrait of the rise and decline of virtuous behavior. This is the question James Q. Wilson raises in a provocative essay,[20] many of whose clues I am here engaged in pursuing. At the time of the Founding, crime was not an issue that much engaged the Founders, although earlier, at the first signs of the rebellion, many feared that any assault upon the authority of the Crown and upon legitimate order, an assault implicit in the very act of rebellion, would unloose a tide of crime. Earlier still, it was not clear to the original settlers, alone in the vastness of a new land, on an "errand in the wilderness," that the God they knew abroad, and the law and civilized reason, would come to prevail in the wildness of this new continent.[21] They had plausible fears that the law of the wilderness might overwhelm them. They knew from the fear in their own hearts what disasters of the spirit might overtake them. The "taming of the West" — of the "badlands" — was an all-too-real concern in the American experience.

Then, following Independence, a tide of crime and incivility and corruption did seem to be rising. In response, from about 1830 onwards, and lasting for more than a century, there was a massive effort at "moral uplift." Through a moral "awakening," the training of "character" was steadily, conscientiously, and extensively prosecuted. And the incidence of crime dropped dramatically. Even during the Depression, despite massive unemployment, despair, grinding poverty, and social dislocation, the incidence of crime remained remarkably low.[22]

This campaign had never been primarily a campaign of "statecraft." Churches and secularists, citizens and associations founded for the task, had pursued it. The long campaign leading to prohibition did, of course, end in an enactment of law, just as the long campaign of Abolition, passing through the bloodiest Civil War in human history, had as its legal fruit Emancipation. The turning of free citizens to government and to law as the means to enforce their vision of character and virtue is, perhaps, natural enough, however wise or unwise in the doing. But government did not lie at the heart of the American effort to build a culture of virtue. What lay at the heart were free associations of individuals, organized for social action, in practicing an ideal of citizenship that consists of not depending upon the state but upon acting for themselves independently of the state.

This century of fruitful social effort demonstrates clearly that a greater reality than the *state*, greater by far both in extension and in power, is the *society*.[23]Society is constituted through those organisms by which free citizens exert their daily acts of conscience and will, quite apart from (although at times also activating) the institutions of the state. Much that the state does not do, or should not do, can be done and is done through the free acts of socially organized citizens.

This crucial point requires emphasis. In the attempt to encourage one another in the practice of virtue, in the effort to inspire one another to shape the highest form of character of which each person is capable, free citizens need not turn to the instrumentalities of the state. In a free society at least, in a society of persons so highly skilled as are the people of the United States in acting through voluntary associatons which they themselves summon into being,[24] citizens have vast capacities for action independently of the state. For more than a hundred years — through the Sunday School movement, through temperance unions, through the Chataqua societies, through the Boy Scouts and Girl Scouts, through the YMCA, through hundreds of associations aimed precisely at teaching character-building and the practice of elementary virtues —

the American people encouraged one another in the pursuit of high civic virtue. Despite wars, depressions, poverty, immense immigration from abroad and vast internal migration; despite the formation of huge cities and industrialization; despite all sorts of social upheaval — crime rates were remarkably low. Society held virtue in esteem, and held crime contemptible. What Tocqueville concluded in 1835 remained true for a century: American *culture* was hostile to crime, and emphatically in favor of virtue.

In America the means available to the authorities for the discovery of crimes and arrest of criminals are few.

There is no administrative police force, and passports are unknown. The criminal police in the United States cannot be compared to that of France; the officers of the public prosecutor's office are few, and the initiative in prosecutions is not always theirs; and the examination of prisoners is rapid and oral. Nevertheless, I doubt whether in any other country crime so seldom escapes punishment.

The reason is that everyone thinks he has an interest in furnishing proofs of an offense and arresting the guilty.

During my stay in the United States I have seen the inhabitants of a county where a serious crime had been committed spontaneously forming committees with the object of catching the criminal and handing him over to the courts.

In Europe the criminal is a luckless man fighting to save his head from the authorities; in a sense the population are mere spectators of the struggle. In America he is an enemy of the human race and every human being is against him.[25]

And then, suddenly, elites began to make fun of virtue and character, temperance and discipline, bourgeois values and "narrow" religion. For nearly fifty years now, an "adversary culture"[26] has grown in power until it has recreated the American *ethos* in its own image.

Those of us who grew up during the 1930s and 1940s can scarcely ignore the great change undergone by the *ethos* of American culture during our lifetime. This change in *ethos* was most marked among elites, especially in the intellectual, literary, and communications fields. Speaking roughly, one might say that once radio, cinema, and other national media of communication began to emerge (during the 1920s), the balance of power among American elites swung slowly but steadily away from the "squares" — from local ministers, local activists, businessmen, and voluntary associations — and towards intellectuals, journalists, filmmakers, and other communicators.[27]

Given the advent of modern communications technology, the class structure of American elites shifted with greater rapidity after World War II. Prior to about 1960, the most honored elite in America was the business class, along with representatives of the established order: doctors (the early Dr. Spock), clergymen (Bishop Sheen, Billy Graham), military officers ("Ike," congressmen with "good military records," such as JFK), and lawmen (J. Edgar Hoover). Professional politicians were held in relatively low repute. After 1960, the symbolic importance of political activism rose dramatically, and new cultural heroes appeared: advance men, speechwriters, the White House staff, "New Frontiersmen" in government agencies, crusading journalists, socially aware actors, writers and filmmakers, academic experts and social activists such as Ralph Nader. In short, the university-trained class of new professionals, trained in skills of organization and communication, began to play a world-historical role. They put a new stamp upon the national *ethos*. Perhaps not all the American public were touched. Certainly, among the elites, there was a pronounced shift in the balance of power toward the makers of our public culture and in its symbolic content; that is, toward the communications elite: in radio, cinema, television, magazines, and the rest.

The general *ethical* direction implicit in this massive swing was a shift from formality to informality, from self-mastery to self-expression, from formation of character to liberation, from virtue to self-discovery. There are many signs that this long swing of the pendulum has reached its outermost angle and will soon begin (if it has not already begun) a slow return.

During this ascendance, one could no longer say with Tocqueville that "in America the criminal is looked upon as an enemy of the human race, and the whole of mankind is against him.'' Those who continued to take the criminal to be an "enemy of the human race" came quite suddenly to be regarded as old-fashioned, unsophisticated, primitive, even fascist. Enlightened persons, by contrast, tried to "understand" the criminal, to regard the criminal as a "victim," and to place unprecedented emphasis upon sympathetic concern for the "rights" of criminals. Correlatively, the same elites began to look upon the forces of government charged with preventing crime as potential agents of abuse, repression, and injustice. Police were called "pigs" by youths, and perhaps the crime then most likely to arouse antagonistic passion was "police brutality." It would be too much to say that in America the *policeman* began to be looked upon "as an enemy of the human race, and the whole of mankind is against him." Some "enlightened" persons, however, did seem to show considerably less sympathy for the police than for those whom the police tried to hold in check.

Behind all these changes lay a new vision of man. According to the traditional American *ethos*, biblical and republican, the imperative given each free person is: "Confirm thy soul in self-control." The American system was regarded as a blessing: "God shed His grace on Thee." According to the new anthropology, two new principles were adduced. First, the American system, as system, is unjust, so that rebellion against it is justified, even necessary for moral liberation. Second, the imperative given each free person is to seek, not self-control, but self-expression. In short, the new imperative of "liberation" required revolt against earlier cultural norms, expectations, systems, and laws. The older *ethos* came suddenly to be regarded as a lower form of morality, to be spurned, ridiculed, and abandoned. In its place was to be built a "new morality," a morality of self-exploration, self-discovery, self-expression, and impulse-release. If the new portrait of the old morality was of a short-haired, buttoned-down, bourgeois, uptight, self-controlled, law-abiding, convention-observing "square," the new symbol of the "new morality" was a long-haired, jean-clad, sandalled, proletarian, groovy, free-spirited, law-defying, convention-flouting "self." The fact that most police are middle-class and many criminals poor fit these symbols neatly. In any conflict between the bourgeoisie and the proletarians, intellectuals would know in advance which side better represents the tide of history.

It would take too long here to show how great historical events during the years 1960-1976 influenced this shift in symbolic allegiances among the new class of communicators. The protests against the war in Vietnam, especially after the Democratic convention of 1968 in Chicago, did shift the sympathies of such paradigmatic figures as Walter Cronkite away from establishment figures such as Hubert Humphrey, Mayor Richard J. Daley, and the Chicago police and toward the rioters in the streets: "our kids" being beaten up by "their kids." Later, the disgracing of such symbols of "law and order" as White House staffers Bob Haldemann and John Erlichman, along with President Richard Nixon in the Watergate trials, served to bring disrepute upon the system of law itself, notwithstanding how that system then worked to mete out justice.

There seem to have been three sources of this massive shift in cultural *ethos*: (1) the symbols of political radicalism; (2) the civil libertarian impulse; and (3) the call of self-expression.

(1) Those who held a leftwing, radical view of the world were exhilarated by such events. The symbols of political radicalism — viz., that, on balance, the U.S. system is a greater force for evil in the world than for good; that a form of domestic as well as international "colonialism" or "imperialism" needs to be countered; and that "wars of liberation" need to be launched at home and abroad — came to influence many symbol-makers and political leaders. In this worldview, any call for law, order, and support for an attack upon crime came to be regarded as a "code word" for repression.[28] It is not so much that anyone was in favor of crime; rather, enlightened persons felt they ought not to give comfort to those reactionaries who "pandered" to the middle-class public's fear of crime.

(2) The civil-libertarian impulse also waxed strong, and without much enlightened opposition. There is a sound American tradition of concern for exact justice and the rights of the accused. The

Declaration of Independence itself indicted the British Crown for abusing the rights of its loyal subjects. Using the strength of this legitimate tradition, and armed with the martyr's delight in opposing public opinion to the contrary, civil libertarians set out to broaden one-sidedly the rights and immunities of those accused of offending law and order. Since rights must always be balanced against rights — the rights of victims against the rights of those accused of victimizing them, e.g. — justice requires due balance. It was not difficult to tip that balance against one side, in favor of the other, when the motive was explicitly one-sided to begin with.

(3) During the period 1960-1976, the cult of self-expression drew upon its roots both in Rousseau and in Hobbes with unprecedented power. From Rousseau, it derived philosophical vindication both for the natural innocence of individuals and for the corruption inherent in the institutions of bourgeois society. From Hobbes, it derived a minimalist view of human liberty, such that human beings ought to be free to indulge in any actions between or among consenting adults, so long as they do not harm the public weal or one another. In this spirit, Abbie Hoffman could *épatez les bourgeoises* by writing: *Steal This Book!* and *Do it!*. Cultural restraints could be regarded as "oppressive." Giving way to internal impulses could be legitimated as "liberation."

By such routes, at least among communications elites and those who chose to live under their influence, the culture of America shifted dramatically away from its early emphasis upon the painstaking acquisition of virtue, the confirmation of the soul in self-control, the pursuit of inner self-mastery, and the formation of character to a new *ethos* of liberation.

If crime follows from a weakening of virtue and character, and especially from a weakening of their supportive cultural *ethos*, then under the new *ethos* and the rejection of the old, one would expect criminal behavior to multiply. And so it did. One would further expect the weakening of the cultural *ethos* to occur with special force among the young, still new to the process of acculturation. And so it did. That, under virtually all cultural conditions, the young between the ages of 15 and 25 belong to the age-cohort most likely to commit crimes of violence would only compound the damage under such new conditions. And so it did. And, finally, that those of the young with the fewest independent resources of socialization — in the family, church, workplace, and neighborhood — would be most under the influence of the *ethos* of the communications media is also to be expected. And so they were.

Among the many possible causes of a widespread practice of virtue and of lives lived according to the dictates of good character, the *ethos* promulgated by important elites via the new instruments of mass communication must be high on the list. The image of a fist raised in defiance became a favorite of the media during the period 1960-76.[29] The metaphors of "letting go,'" "born free," and "liberation" became powerful symbols in the lives of millions. It is hard to think of any countervailing symbols of self-discipline, the acquisition of virtue, and character that were given equal public weight during that period.[30]

Two final observations are necessary. The use of the novel dominant *ethos* of the period 1960-1976 for partisan political purposes may not have been entirely cynical. But it must be observed that such symbols did in fact serve the purposes of leftwing politics. Even Jimmy Carter, whose sudden prominence was in large measure due to the fact that he was a practicing Sunday School teacher and a "born again Christian," the very embodiment of the old biblical, republican, rural *ethos* of the nation, and for that reason able to deliver a large part of the South to the left, found it expedient to be championed by *Rolling Stone*, to give an interview in *Playboy*, to build his campaign around concerts by rock stars, and in many other ways to make himself the candidate also of the new *ethos* and of its paradigmatic figures. One can say that, given Jimmy Carter's attachment to Sunday School virtue, the public tide began to turn in 1976. Yet even Jimmy Carter had to pay the "new morality" its due — and paid the price of defeat in 1980.

Moreover, the new morality wrought special havoc in the black community especially in urban areas. Rural black culture still retains powerful means of socialization in virtue and character. Families tend to be stronger. Churches tend to be a dominant influence. The inroads of modern communications tend to be correspondingly weaker. The American black community tends to be one of the most *conservative* in terms of the old morality. The regular teaching of virtue and character through traditional means of socialization, however, is far weaker in urban areas, and the power of the new means of communication is far stronger. Yet during the period 1960-1976, the American black population was experiencing the great and admirable "civil rights revolution." For blacks, especially, there was true social relevance to the cry: "Free at last! Free at last! Thank God Almighty, free at last!" The symbols of that revolution, in fact, were symbols of extraordinary virtue, extraordinary strength of character, and extraordinary social discipline. Non-violent resistance is the very opposite of "letting go" and "free-expression." It is a triumph of character.

Nonetheless, this noble movement among black Americans — during which they moved from being self-described as "Negro Americans" to "black Americans" or "Afro-Americans" — evoked an ambivalent response among communications elites. On the one hand, few could be unsympathetic to the great drama of moral achievement on the part of Martin Luther King, Jr., and the civil rights movement. On the other hand, few dared to treat blacks as critically and objectively as they treat other groups in society. The emotional solution to this ambivalence was to treat black Americans on virtually all occasions as *victims*, under the moral imperative: "Thou shalt not blame the victim."[31] That this was patronizing and, in its own way, racist did not prevent its routine occurrence. Thus, in enlightened commentary even blacks convicted as criminals evoked understanding, sympathy, and excuses. This rhetorical solution deprived law-abiding blacks of any credit for virtue and character. And it undermined in the world of mass communications any attempt to reinforce those who, isolated and alone, still insisted upon the crucial human need for virtue and character.

As George Gilder pointed out in his powerful but little-read *Visible Man*,[32] the most visible of all Americans during the period 1960-1976 (on magazine covers, in books, in front-page articles, and on television shows) was the black militant, typically with fist clenched and voicing defiance. The most invisible were the millions of hardworking, virtuous, quietly advancing, and determined black workers, entrepreneurs, and professionals. The media loved the few defiant ones; it ignored the majority. (That this is in itself a kind of racism, and probably a subjective projection, was long overlooked.) Communications elites were thereby promoting one *ethos*, diminishing another. Did this have no effect at all?

For one thing, this mass-produced public image badly injured the public reputation of black Americans as a whole. For another, it tended to confuse militance for good causes with criminality, as if both were equally symptoms of "oppression." I visited one university during the early 1970s whose administration claimed to be promoting civil rights by insisting in its affirmative action program that the recruiters bring in "street" blacks, even with criminal records, definitely *not* "middle class" blacks. The president proudly asserted that he wished to help the "truly oppressed." The havoc his college later experienced need not be detailed.

During the years 1960-1976, criminal acts by black youths multiplied to historically unprecedented proportions. Some commentators have countered that there is "oppression" even in the fact that blacks are disproportionately represented in America's prison population. Few argue that such persons are entirely innocent of crime, only that they are more aggressively pursued and arrested. It is possible that this is true. But there are some studies of violent personal crime that do not derive from arrest records, but from interviews with victims, even in cases in which no arrests have been made. By higher proportions than their percentage of the population as a whole, the victims of violent crime are black. When such victims identify by race the person who victimized them, the perpetrators are also disproportionately black, by an even higher disproportion.[33] These figures show, also, that personal violent crime in the United States is disproportionately perpetrated by blacks. They oblige those who know such statistical information to find an explanation for it. There are many such. To go into them would take us too far afield. The point for present purposes is that, to this point, this information is seldom discussed in public by communications elites, although it is widely discussed in private. This disjunction between public and private discussion cannot be healthy. It is, however, another evidence of the rhetorical ambivalence mentioned above.

4. TOWARD A CULTURAL RESPONSE TO CRIME

As the attentive reader will have discerned, the argument so far leads us to a powerful conclusion. *Cultural elites can mount an effective campaign against crime by helping to shape a cultural* ethos *which regards the criminal as "an enemy of the human race," and by amassing evidence that "the whole of mankind is against him."* By this, I do not wish to assert that a powerful anti-crime cultural *ethos* will alone suffice in eliminating crime. Under virtually any *ethos*, there will be crime. (There have been criminal acts even within monasteries: Not too many years ago, one monk murdered another at St. John's Abbey in Collegeville, Minnesota.) My thesis is more limited: Among many other social factors, the power of the prevailing cultural *ethos* has considerable importance.

This thesis cries out for a more positive formulation: *A cultural* ethos *inculcating in every citizen the need for the acquisition of virtue, the imperatives of self-control and self-mastery, and the moral obligation to assume responsibility for the painstaking shaping of one's own character, will significantly decrease the frequency of criminal acts.* I do not think this thesis can be overturned.

Consider, for example, its direct denial. Let someone say that the prevailing cultural *ethos* has *no* effect upon the frequency of crime. Such an assertion would require believing that each individual tempted to commit a crime would receive only such weak signals from the opinions of others, such weak response from institutions, and such license to self-respect and self-justification despite the views and actions of others, that he or she could be wholly indifferent to them. Such an objection would be easy to hold when the prevailing cultural *ethos* is quite permissive about crime. But if the opposite is the case, social retribution is likely to be swift. Consult again the quotation from Tocqueville cited above.

Consider next the objection that, even if the prevailing cultural *ethos* imposes the "tyranny" of "bourgeois values," rebellious persons would still commit crimes, as if in brave defiance. No doubt this is true. But two considerations deserve attention. First, the objection now entertains the difference between individuals who simply drift with the crowd and conform to prevailing doctrine, and those who have the "bravery" to stand in defiance. Surely the proportion in the latter category is, in any society, smaller than the proportion in the former. Secondly, this objection supposes that a regimen of virtue, self-control, and character must be imposed from above by "tyranny." It need not be. If it is as natural for humans to choose virtue as vice, as natural to choose self-control as impulse-release, and as natural to choose character as dissolution, then perhaps significant proportions of human beings can be persuaded of their own free choice to choose the first set of alternatives rather than the second. James Q. Wilson cites Thomas W. Laqueur as showing for England, in a portrait apparently as true for the United States, that the Sunday School movement, which in many places reached half or more of the population, cut across all class lines. Through it and movements like it, "the bourgeois world view triumphed in the nineteenth century largely through consent, not through force."[34] It is one of the givens of character-building that it can only be achieved through voluntary, chosen, and steadily pursued "self-actualization."

The more telling objection is likely to leave standing the heart of the thesis, while attacking only its feasibility. Yes, the objector may advance, a cultural *ethos* committed to character-building is likely to diminish the frequency of criminal acts. *But* the United States of the 1980s is never going to go back to "the old-time religion" or "the bourgeois order." This objection might well be voiced not only by a person who objects personally to the voluntary regimen of virtue, self-discipline and character, but precisely by someone committed to those values who despairs of ever seeing them regain their prominence in these United States. (There are conservatives who delight in predicting gloom and doom.)

No doubt, the wise response to this objection is simply to re-state the thesis, because it is true. And one might then add: "Too bad for the United States; cultures decline as well as rise; so went ancient Rome, etc." Despite being of somber and melancholic Slavic background, however, I find such *Weltschmerz* unrealistic. Consider a few trivial points: (1) If I recall correctly, only 15 years ago fewer than a million Americans were regular joggers; by 1984, the number was 30 million. If this is not a major change, not only in *ethos*, but in ascetic discipline, what is? (2) Between 1830 and 1850 per capita alcohol consumption in the U.S. is calculated to have fallen, under the impact of various temperance movements, from 7.1 gallons per year to 1.8 gallons.[35] (3) During the past twenty years, the feminist movement is credited with winning rather immense and sweeping changes in American values, attitudes, and practices. Even these three examples, among many others, suggest that no one can plausibly hold that *all* fairly broad and rapid social change is impossible. So perhaps the objection must be recast so as only to hold that *this particular* social change is impossible. Impossible? Even that would be too strong. Unlikely? Even that may be doubted.

Why, on the face of it, would it be more difficult to move forward in the direction of an *ethos* of impulse-restraint than it was during preceding decades to move in the direction of an *ethos* of impulse-release? If one replies that a move in the direction of impulse-release is more like pandering, whereas a move in the direction of impulse-restraint requires effort and discipline, one merely surrenders. Does anyone dare to argue, on philosophical grounds, that a *lack* of self-activating, self-regulating, all-purpose inner control represents a higher stage of human development than its attainment? Dare one argue today in favor of lack of character? Does anyone really hold that the human being is by spontaneous instinct solely innocent, sweet, other-regarding, and civilized?

The American people have had considerable experience over the past twenty years with virtually untrammelled liberty, openness, and self-expression. They have learned, to their regret, that when some persons are free to express themselves, they mug, rape, and kill. It seems as native to some to be barbarous as to be civilized. When some persons seek instant self-gratification, they — like two men in California recently — indulge themselves in the torturing, mutilation, and murder of helpless victims (filming all this on videotape the while). True, every human alive has felt the *impulse* to steal what does not belong to him (such that God could properly count as of universal relevance His commandments: "Thou shalt not steal" and "Thou shalt not covet"). Some, alas, vigorously nourish that impulse, do covet, and do steal.

It will not do to say that those whose habitual forms of self-expression are criminal are "sick," or "oppressed," or "victims." For some, of course, it may be true that their conduct is wholly and moment-to-moment beyond their own control; as physical deformities are relatively frequent among human beings, so, surely, there are some who suffer permanent and irretrievable moral deformities, through no fault of their own. But others clearly indicate by their patterns of action a sufficient degree of reasoning and choice, purposiveness and caution, to suggest that they choose when they will exercise their criminal habits and how. It is this segment of the class of habitual criminals, presumably, in which frequencies of crime may be increased or decreased through various efforts by society as a whole. This is the population that is the proper focus of this essay.

To suggest that all in this class are incapable of moral choice, and not responsible for their own actions, is to take away from them their humanity. By contrast, to affirm the contrary, i.e., to say that they behave immorally, is to grant them human dignity. Further, if it is a norm of human action that persons *ought* to perform their actions out of moral choice and to assume responsibility for them, then it follows that they require a settled, permanent, all-purpose disposition to do so. In a word, they require "character." They will need to have mastered the moral skills — the acquired virtues — requisite to making free, informed, and consensual choices. It will then be expected of every adult man or woman that he or she is responsible for forming his or her own character through mastery of the virtues requisite for the exercise of moral liberty.

It is, of course, possible for a reasonable person to object (as some in Plato's dialogues did object):

"Whatever others may do, *I* do not choose to live a life of virtue, self-mastery, and character." One can make that choice. One can even live accordingly. But what one cannot do, plausibly, is make an argument for that choice. One may live immorally, even *choose* to live immorally. But a human being cannot give a reasoned argument for so doing. For the exercise of the habits of the heart and mind necessary to present a reasoned argument requires the virtues, self-mastery, and character one is intending to deny. Argue, if you will, without honesty, at whim, and as impulse moves you. Be self-expressive to your self's content. When you attempt to conduct an argument in a civilized, reasoned fashion, honoring the dignity of the person with whom you argue, you must rise considerably above self-indulgence, impulse-release, and mere self-expressiveness. "Hell," Jean-Paul Sartre once wrote, "is other people." For those whose universe is bound by ego, so it is. It is quite otherwise for those who love civilization, the constitutive act of which is reasoned conversation with other persons.

5. A DISCOURSE ON LIBERTY

It is one of the advantages of the Aristotelian-Thomistic worldview that its conception of liberty involves the conception of liberty's constitutive skills. In certain other philosophies, emphasis falls upon the absence of coercion (especially by the state). Liberty is therein conceived of as indeterminate. So long as one is not coerced, one is free.

This is a bare-bones, almost empty notion. Against it is the fact that there are many things I am not free to do, not because I am under coercion, but because I lack the relevant skills. No one forces me not to speak Spanish (as I would like to do), but I am not now free to do so, given past failures to master the relevant skills. For Aristotle, and even more for Aquinas, liberty is conceived of in terms of its enabling skills. This is a far richer conception of liberty, and morally of much greater relevance. To gain one's liberty, some say, one must throw off bonds imposed by an oppressor. For Aristotle and Aquinas, that part is too simple. From that point on, liberty must be gained as an inner discipline whose constitutive skills are many.

The normal course of human life exhibits this process well-enough. The infant, so far as state coercion goes, is as free a citizen in a free society as are its parents. It is not free, however, to do all that they can do. Even at the age of seven, or whenever it is that the child grows able to reason and to make choices for reasons stronger than impulse, the child is not yet accomplished enough to exercise the range of liberty attained by its parents. So also with the adolescent, partly child still and partly adult, uncertain of his or her identity, judgment, and even mood, not yet comfortable with the responsibilities of adulthood but resentful of the restrictions of childhood. And even among adults, who at twenty has the range of acquired skills he will have at thirty, at forty, at fifty, or later? During a full human life there is considerable room to grow in liberty.

Happiness, Aristotle wrote, thinking of the achievement of virtue, *requires* a long life.[36]

Criminal law incorporates the Aristotelian-Thomistic conception of liberty in its conceptions of responsibility, intent, premeditation, and the like. It recognizes that not every action by a man is a human action. An inadvertent act, an impulsive act, an unintended act — these have, for criminal law, a different weight from fully human actions, framed with due knowledge and due deliberation, and executed accordingly. I do not here wish to assess the philosophy of man implicit in criminal law. My present subject is not the law but liberty. What I am trying to bring to light is our common, shared awareness of the often unnoticed reality that liberty is a far from empty concept. In order to be a free act, a human action must involve the actualization of several moral skills which are not always in operation. Absent-mindedly kicking sand with our toes while lying on the beach, dozing and only half-aware of anything at all, we are not quite up to being free agents. Our liberty must be exercised from inside-out. And that typically requires getting ourselves up for the event: awake, alert, attentive, considering, judging, matching means to ends, and deciding to act.

"Competent" to stand trial; "able to distinguish good from evil", "insane at the moment of the crime"; "blinded by passion" — such locutions, whose exact legal bearing I mean carefully to avoid, suggest that the law has ample experience of the depth and complexity of the human psyche.

In this respect, an apparent conflict is often remarked between the legal approach to crime, rooted in concepts of freedom and responsibility, and the approach of the social sciences to crime. Clearly, though, discussions of freedom vs. determinism in scientific literature, not least in the treatment of crime, often pose a false autonomy. As Wilson and Herrnstein put it in *Crime and Human Nature*, scientific advances in the study of human behavior may gradually be able to identify the whole range of causes, biological and environmental, which "explain" such behavior without reference to human liberty, while, nonetheless, our system of criminal law and criminal justice proceeds, and must proceed, on crucial assumptions about liberty.[37] Are these two tendencies irreconcilable? There are two reasons for thinking they are not.

The assumptions of the system of criminal justice are compatible with, if not derivative from, the presuppositions of Jewish and Christian tradition. In that tradition, it is assumed that *God* knows all the causes of human behavior. God knows "what is in man," sees into "the darkest recesses of the heart," and "nothing is unknown to Him." The fact that human behavior is wholly intelligible is not then, at least in the founding assumptions of Western civilization, inconsistent with human liberty. (I leave aside here the puzzle theologians struggle over; viz., how God can *know* something, efficaciously *know* it, without causing it to happen, thus destroying human liberty. Many solutions have been offered.[38] Scientists are not involved in exactly the same perplexity. Scientists may seek omniscience; omnipotence is not their realm.)

The second reason is that, in the Jewish and Christian tradition, it is an error to think of human beings as *simply* free. Many are (indeed, all of us are at least some of the time) "slaves to their passions," "bonded to 'this world' and its deceptions," "unfree." Thus, both in the secular vision of Aristotle and in the religious visions of the authors of the Jewish and Christian Testaments, human beings are less to be described as free and more to be described as *capable* of freedom, seekers after freedom, trying to become free. Those, for example, who are totally under the sway of "the spirit of this world," the *ethos* of their own era, their peers, their friends, and their families are not quite to be regarded as *free*. Free they may be in principle and in potency; they are far from having seized, appropriated, and begun living according to their own liberty in act. Human beings need to achieve liberty through an arduous process of self-actualization, a combat, a struggle against themselves (and against powers greater than themselves), a "Pilgrim's Progress" notable for its hazards, defeats, long labors, and dangers. In short, a great deal of "determinism" is conceded, against which the seeker after liberty must struggle.

This picture, then, is not inconsistent with what both human experience and social science (even at its current stage of incompleteness) already show us. All persons do act by "necessities" which they did not choose, barely understand, and find difficult, if not impossible, to resist. Long before a person comes of an age in which he or she is capable of such self-consciousness as is sufficient for self-direction, each has been "thrown" into history, along a trajectory not of the self's own making. Never are human beings in circumstances thoroughly of their own foreseeing or arranging or beyond influences which powerfully affect the choices open to them. Nonetheless, heightened self-consciousness does, from time to time, show us how our behavior in past circumstances has been less than free, and how we might teach ourselves to break through such unconscious patterns in the future. Giving way habitually to an explosive temper, we might come to learn the sorts of stimuli that typically bring us to explosion, prepare ourselves to counter them, and gain at least some measure of mastery over them. And similarly with many other impulsive, instinctive, and habitual reactions.

Therefore, it is quite consistent to say that no one is *wholly* free, and yet to measure persons by the *degree* of self-mastery they have to this point attained. (To "confirm thy soul in self-control" is to appropriate one's proper liberty as an autonomous human being.) Moreover, at every stage of life there are degrees of self-mastery humans have a right to expect of one another. One expects more of teenagers than of children; more of seasoned persons than of young adults. One expects no one to be perfect. Properly to be expected is that measure of self-mastery which, at the very least, prevents a person from serious criminal offenses against others.

In short, there are *degrees* of freedom. The proper measure is not "all or nothing." Furthermore, there is a high *social* interest in expecting of each other, first, that minimum responsibility for one's own actions that keeps one from crime (as well as from other non-criminal behaviors that would make social life impossibly difficult). There is, second, an important social interest in expecting of each other that striving towards perfection that meets the highest levels aspired to by our civilization: levels witnessed to by the saints, by the wise men and the valiant women whose example we rightly commemorate. A society's moral dynamism depends on its commitment to the struggle for perfection, however unattainable.

Liberty and science, then, are not at war. Indeed, the findings of science are of great utility to those who seek to understand why they are as they are, in order to gain from self-knowledge the ability to choose among the many influences that in fact impinge upon them. Naturally, no person can resist all the influences, within and without, that condition his humanity. Humans are not angels, but embodied persons, creatures of time, earthbound, and weak. Self-knowledge, therefore, has two parts to it. It is, in part, self-discovery: learning what one's own basic material is, within and without. This constitutes the natural endowment within which each works out his vocation. But self-knowledge is also, in part, self-invention: deciding among those possibilities open to us which ones we shall choose to reinforce, which to resist. William James liked to call attention to the simple fact that at every single moment our consciousness is bombarded by a "blooming, buzzing" confusion, to only some of whose superabundant stimuli we can actually pay attention.[39] Yet, not unlike a stabbing light in a surrounding abyss, we are remarkably free moment-to-moment, with respect to *where* we direct our attention. Concentration is the defining trait of character, and the root of human liberty.

6. CHARACTER AND CRIME

As a means for satisfying desire, crime sometimes appears to be both so attractive and so "rational" that one must wonder why crimes do not occur more frequently. What does it take for citizens *not* to commit crimes? Why, for example, does not shoplifting appeal to ninety-nine percent of the population, instead of to a tiny fraction? It is possible that, for some, fear is sufficient motive: fear of punishment, fear of consequences, fear of violating the law. If desire is an accelerator, fear is a brake. Let us examine each of these fears in turn.

Fear of punishment. For some persons, two sorts of punishment have been envisaged: punishment by society in this life, and punishment by the all-knowing Almighty in the next. Psychologically, however, desire focusses on a good that is immediate, concrete, and tangible, whereas fear focusses upon a threat more distant, abstract, and presently invisible. Further, punishment may be neither certain nor swift. (It may not even be commensurate with the good to be achieved.) Further, a lively sense of "the fear of God" is typically achieved only through a considerable effort of reflection and a long orientation of one's life toward matters invisible, "hoped for, but unseen." In a word, the power of fear derives not a little of its force from the surrounding cultural *ethos*, its institutions, and its practices.

The problem for virtue, however, is that a very free society, which allows its citizens much private space for the development of their own psychic orientations, tends to relax the fear both of social and of divine punishment. Within it, the aggressive, gratification-centered ego has considerable room for growth. In earlier eras of history, too, spiritual masters recognized that the fear of punishment, while gross, vulgar and broad in its popular appeal, is ultimately a weak motivating force, since it comes as it were from outside-in. It does not affix itself to the center of the self; it is an external check. The self is likely to struggle to "overcome" fear, in the name (perhaps falsely assumed) of self-determination.

Finally, those whose capacity to imagine the future is weak are likely to be less moved by fear of later punishment, than are those whose consciousness is habitually future-directed. Thus, if morality is partly constituted by an orientation towards responsibility for one's own future, the paradox is that those more easily moved by the fear of punishment are less likely to require fear as their motive, since more positive goals of self-mastery already attract them. Still, one should not underestimate the power of fear of punishment for those who measure life by the gratification of desire. Brute animals are "trained" through fear of pain and the reward of pleasure, rationally applied by their trainer. The closer to the capacities of their animal nature cunning humans live, the more they are likely to need fear, rather than reason, as their guide.

Fear of consequences. To commit a crime is to commit oneself to a new order of being and doing: an order beyond the legal (and the moral) order. It is to enter the unknown territory of the outlaw. In both realms, though, consequences are not likely to be orderly in the same sense as in the world of law and moral order. In that realm, others are likely to treat one as one treats others. As there is a golden rule, so there is also an iron rule. Hobbes was not wrong to imagine that there is, in each human psyche, at least a primal awareness of a possible world of nightmarish violent anarchy. Images of unpredictable vengeance in "gangland wars" and "drug wars" are sufficiently vivid in modern societies to permit many to sense that to commit a crime is to invite unforeseeable threats against their own survival. Not far from human consciousness, then, is a dim sense that personal survival is linked to the world of law and moral order. To violate that world is to become vulnerable to unforeseeable consequences of a vaguely terrifying kind. Hobbes might describe it as an intuition of "the war of all against all."

Fear of violating the law. In a normally well-ordered society, children are taught from their earliest days to respect the law and the moral order. One overhears in a playground their cries against injustice, cheating, unfairness, aggression, and greed; one hears their insistence upon exact fidelity to rules. It may not even be too much to posit an innate sense of justice and fairness in the young, often indeed more extreme and abstract and ruthless than among their elders. Thus, Aristotle was obliged to remark that the young are not ready fully to understand ethics because, lacking experience of life, they tend to understand ethics solely in terms of abstract rules. The young have not had time to acquire the necessary sense of how the moral life entails not only a multiplicity of rules but, even more important, a proper perception of the moral demands imposed by unique concrete circumstances. For Aristotle, acting well depends upon a slowly learned instinct for how to do the right thing, in the right way, at the right time, with the right touch.[40]

Nonetheless, whether among the young or among their elders, respect for the law, because it is the law, instills in many a fear of violating it: not precisely out of fear of punishment or fear of unknown evil consequences, but out of fear of violating the respect that the law deserves. For the law — not solely the law of the Republic but also the natural law and the divine law, (which the

former is held, however imperfectly, to approx-
imate) — is properly an object of respect and even
of love. The law is even an object of self-love (a
powerful love indeed), since the purpose of the law
is to protect one's own survival. Thus, many have
rightly been taught, and have taught themselves,
never knowingly to violate the law. Such persons
are called "law-abiding," and sometimes even
"God-fearing," since for many human law is a
reflection of God's love and will. One should not
underestimate the sacredness attached by many
citizens to law; one should not underestimate their
love for it. One may read in the Psalms a great many
eloquent expressions of such respect and such love.

Beyond fear, however, there are many other
motives for avoiding criminal acts. Many citizens,
for example, embrace as the story they mean to live
out in their lives a project of self-mastery and self-
control (as in the words of the traditional American
hymn earlier cited). They understand by liberty a
life of impulse-restraint. While it is true that their
desires and impulses solicit them in many directions, they try to school themselves toward acting
with deliberation and restraint.

Some do this by shaping their conduct according
to rules. Others use such rules as if for training, but
regard the moral life less as a matter of abiding by
ethical rules than as a matter of shaping their actions to meet their inward image of how a noble,
beautiful person would act. In this respect, there
are *several* different traditions of moral formation
in Western thought, several more, in fact, than are

typically taught in the philosophy departments of our better universities. Well-known to academics are the Kantian tradition, the utilitarian tradition (including "act-utilitarianism" and "rule-utilitarianism"), but these do not exhaust the moral repertoire of American citizens. Philosophically, the traditions of existentialism and personalism (put to such good use by Pope John Paul II), the traditions of Aristotelianism and Thomism, and the ethical teachings of American pragmatists, and the teachings of the Talmud and the rabbis — to name but a few — approach the moral life in ways quite different from those of Kant and Bentham. Sound scholarship ought not to overlook, then, the many *communities* of moral discourse, common to which is significant instruction in the paths of self-control.

It should be unnecessary to point out, but in the present state of ethical discussion perhaps it is useful to point out, that all such traditions, each in its own way, appeals to an underlying understanding of human moral psychology. Speaking roughly, as one must do in generalizing about such disparate traditions, the human psyche is commonly regarded as a focal point for whose attention many inward factions compete: desire and fear, ambition and aggression, conflicting appetites and passions, memory and imagination, a sense of self and a sense of others, reasonableness and will — all of these in mutual (and mortal) combat. The moral question, all see, is a question of psychic ordering. How each person organizes his or her inner life in response to life's minute-by-minute demands for action defines that person's character. Since each person begins with a unique genetic endowment and a unique environment (e.g., even one's position as first-born or middle child or youngest makes a difference), possibilities of variation are infinite. Restraining some impulses, nurturing others, are activities no human being can avoid. But *which* impulses they restrain, and *which* they encourage, tells the tale of their lives. This very circumstance led St. Thomas Aquinas to hazard that one way in which the human race is "made in the image of God" is by reflecting His infinity through its endless individual variation.

Given this background, it may be hypothesized that the criminal character is shaped by the characteristic nurturing of certain impulses, to the neglect of others. It is not difficult to see that every human person may sometime, out of "weakness" (even by his or her own lights), commit a serious crime. The virtuous ordering of one's life all the time, every day, and without fail is a very tall order. (Is it not amazing that crime is not more frequent than it is?) But experience suggests that there is an important difference between a criminal guilty of a single lapse, in an otherwise unblemished life ("There but for the grace of God ..."), and an habitual criminal, committed to a life (or at least a significant period of a life) of crime. It does not seem farfetched to hold that habitual criminals nourish in themselves (or are limited to) a certain range of impulses and tendencies. Among the habits one would expect to find encouraged and given a long leash: to aggression, to treating other persons as means rather than as ends, to self-deception and rationalization, and to imagining that it is the ego's right to take or to seize what the ego desires.

What sort of character is required, then, if one is *not* to commit crime? We have already mentioned the possibilities of a character formed around three different sorts of fear. What can be said in a more positive way? Again (a trinitarian to the bitter end), let me mention three requirements: First, one must be willing to restrain such impulses as result in criminal acts. Second, one must respect others as ends, not solely as means. Third, one must be honest about one's own purposes, weaknesses, and modest place in a universe of other persons.

Impulse-restraint. No doubt, the person who has never felt murderous rage, or the impulse to take what is not his or hers, or the impulse to hurt others cruelly (even physically) is a very rare person indeed. When a person commits criminal acts from impulsions such as these, that person is not less "human." Still, one properly sees in such acts significant defects of virtue. To give way to impulses of this sort is to not only to fail to exercise due restraint but also to enter into war against others. Acts fed by such impulses make civilized life ultimately impossible; persons unconstrained by reason must be restrained by force. Civilization entails rule by law and by reason. The *out*law is indeed outside the law that makes civilization possible.

Respect for persons as ends. A life governed by

law has as its premise the dignity of human persons as agents of law and of reason. The end served by law is to secure the integrity of the human persons. Two classic texts assert as much: "But man is by no means for the State. The State is for man" (J. Maritain[41]); second, "To secure these rights, governments are instituted among men ...." Human persons command respect (are *dignus*: L., worthy) because they are originating agents of inquiry, insight, judgment, and choice. These are the actions humans perform (alone among the creatures of this earth) as properly their own. To violate these human capacities is to violate their highest and specific nature. To violate them in another is to wrong these others by treating them as less than they are, and to reduce them to the status of being slaves of the criminal's own purposes, mere objects at the criminal's "legitimate" disposal.

We speak even of the things people own as *property*, that is, things *proper* to them, part of their own identity, physical extensions of their own liberty, through which they express their identity in the world of fact. To violate a person's property is to violate that person in the root of his or her earthly liberty. That is why a burglary committed even in a person's absence leaves the victim feeling psychically violated: his things are part of him. Even more obviously in acts of violence against a person's body, the criminal reduces others to means for his own gratification. This act of self-aggrandizement may make a criminal seem to himself almost omnipotent, master of all the others ("a master criminal"). Yet, paradoxically, such a violation of other persons also reduces the criminal's own status. If other human beings are not ends, neither is he. The criminal thereby annihilates his own dignity. Reducing human life to a game of power, he reduces it to the status of brutes. Ironically, by his own failure to develop morally at a pace consistent with his physical development, he may in fact (secretly) regard himself as of zero moral worth, and be inflicting his own self-evaluation upon others. He thereby imposes his false reality upon the world of others.

Thus, the moral universe of the criminal is a sort of unreality. The universe he must create for himself as the proscenium of his daily actions is a fiction. In his world, there is a war of all against all, and power alone matters. In his world, his ego fights against nothingness and chaos, establishing itself as the center of gratification, around which other persons revolve like satellites to be used at his pleasure. So great is this unreality that in the real world outside him, whose secret springs he does not grasp, he must live by his wits. The practices of civilization serve many of his purposes, and he will use them as a disguise and a mask until he wishes to strike. His craft lies in catching his victims by surprise, appealing to the rules of civilization until he is ready to rip off the mask and do his will. Civilization, he may think, is made to serve his will. He may easily fantasize that he is its master. All of it exists to serve him.

It is exactly here that the "insanity defense" is so

mischievous. In a certain respect, the habitual criminal does live in a world of unreality. In his universe, his ego is god. That is not the way it is in the real world. One can, therefore, look at all criminal conduct as "insane." No "rational" person, we find ourselves saying, could act as he does. In a more powerful sense, though, we may ask why many more other human beings do not choose to be outlaws, to live in an ego-centered and impulse-directed universe of their own creation, within which other persons are never (or rarely) ends but only means. This is surely an option for human liberty. It can be freely chosen. The characterology supporting it can be purposefully — or even lazily, almost inadvertently — nourished. In this sense, we see clearly enough that those who choose such a self-definition must be made to face its implications: They have chosen to be less than human, to violate their own nature as persons in a universe of ends, and to enslave themselves to their own demanding, destructive, self-diminishing egos. They are not insane; they have willingly misconstrued their own nature. They have deform-ed themselves.

To treat as "ill" persons who have chosen to live a life of habitual crime, as if they were victims of something outside themselves, is itself to treat criminals as victims, not as persons; as slaves, not as free men; as means, not as ends. It is, in a peculiar way, to accept the same universe and the same picture of reality as the criminals do, only to label it differently. This is why therapy based upon the concept that criminals are "ill" mirrors the criminal's own way of thinking, except that the criminal is likely, in simple self-respect, to re-letter the signposts. If systems, persons, and events outside himself are responsible for making him "ill," treating him as a means to ends he neither fathoms nor chooses, then he has been correct all along. Life *is* a "war of all against all," in which freedom and personal responsibility, and a self-image as being an end and not solely a means, have nothing to do with him. Blind forces deserve blind responses. His life has been justified.

The only therapy that matters, in such a case, is that the criminal be led to see that he is not "ill," but that he has made a terrifying mistake. He must learn that it lies within his power to see how thoroughly mistaken, how other-destructive and how self-destructive, he has been. Somehow, somewhere, the criminal misconstrued reality and began to form his habits to fantasies. Generically, the criminal is like the rest of us and must submit to the same inner disciplines. All of us are led by fantasies; in shattering them, reality is our constant teacher. Aristotle held that for the learning of virtue a long life is required, since in each of us at every stage much fantasy remains to be stripped away by hard experience. Fortunately, the unrealistic images most citizens are prey to are not criminal, and their education in virtue helps them earlier to avoid being quite so destructive, either of others or of themselves. The criminal is not exempt from the universal human need to bend intellect and will to the grain and the contours of instruction in reality. He too must take up the common human burden, joining the rest of us.

Honesty vs. self-deception. The habitual criminal cannot live as he lives without constant self-deception. His nature as a rational being obliges him to justify his conduct. He will offer abundant (and often strikingly inventive) reasons for it. His capacities for rationalization are, and must be, finely honed, since he must daily explain, if only to himself, why he does not behave as others do. Moreover, his craft, such as it may be, also obliges him to become skillful in the ways of deception, not only of others but also of himself. "I'm not going to hurt you, ma'am," he may even say with kindness. "Just do as I say, and nothing will happen. Don't do anything foolish, and everything will be okay." So saying, he deftly switches responsibility to the other person — the victim — as if some action by that victim might perfectly justify any violence he might be "forced" to perpetrate. This is thorough self-deception. It may well be the case that the robber or the rapist does not want bloodshed (only the goods or the body of the other), and intends to avoid it. But robbery and rape are already acts of violence; they already exhibit contempt for the victim.

Self-deception may run very deep. The habitual criminal is likely, often and perhaps always, to walk away from a crime in a glow almost equivalent to a virtuous glow. He is likely to feel good about himself, superior, masterful. He got what he wanted, perhaps with a minimum of "trouble," and with as few "complications" as possible. To imagine a habitual criminal stricken with grief and torn by a guilty conscience seems contrary to abundant testimony. Still, common sense does lead us to use the word "hardened" to distinguish between those whose criminality still has some limits and those who have settled comfortably into their own world of unreality.

Thus, habitual criminals daily afford elaborate self-justifications to arresting officers, newspaper reporters, one another, and seasoned therapists or counselors. Some draw odd lines — they mention certain crimes *they* would never indulge in — as if to signal their own moral superiority. Honor does survive even among thieves. Human beings can scarcely be expected to act in habitual ways without having a moral theory for what they do, a parroted rationalization, which they will expect others to find as convincing as they do. Such tribute is exacted of criminals, to be paid to the world of law, to moral order, and to reason itself.

Moreover, in a society as free and pluralistic as ours, no one overarching moral tradition is appealed to by all. There is, therefore, ample room for a highly personal version of the moral universe. In our sort of society the criminal is quite likely to work up an account in which he stands justified. To oblige him to confront the full implications of his reasoning, spelled out so as to apply equally to all other persons, would require long and tedious work, during which he is likely to spot multiple opportunities for turning dialectics toward self-justification. One of his more common methods may be to concede that, yes, he "broke" the law — as if "the law" were an external limit, having nothing to do with his standing as a person, as if breaking it were like a child inadvertently stepping on a crack in a sidewalk. That he got caught, while so many others known to him still go free, may even stir his own indignation at being singled out unjustly.

In such ways, it does not seem that even habitual criminals lack a sense of justice, rights, or moral standing. Nowadays, their public rhetoric, at least, often appeals to such concepts. Are habitual criminals likely to condemn their own behavior in the light of these concepts? To do so would require of them a massive reorientation of their own habits.

Because the criminal is likely to identify the law as a barrier to his freedom, he is likely to imagine that in breaking through it he is, unlike others, supremely free. This is fools' fire. Liberty is won within, by a victory of parts of oneself over other parts of oneself, in that "inner combat" that constitutes the struggle for virtue. Declining that combat, the habitual criminal condemns himself to a childlike moral life: to that half-life of self-deception and impulse-gratification, combined with contempt for his fellowman, which defines a state of moral underdevelopment.

Similarly, the widely cited phenomenon of recidivism clearly signals deficient liberty. It suggests — it screams aloud — that a man is still not under his own control, is still lacking in self-mastery and its inherent freedom to choose. Thinking of power over others, and priding himself on his manhood, the habitual criminal presents quite the opposite spectacle. He has long resisted the struggle for moral manhood. Others equally disadvantaged, equally armed with potential excuses, have not declined it.

Since I write as a philosopher and theologian rather than as a social scientist, I am loathe to cite the literature of social science on such matters as though I know it thoroughly; I do not. Yet three judgments of Dr. Samenow are immediately apposite:

> The criminal values people only insofar as they bend to his will or can be coerced or manipulated into doing what he wants. He has been this way since childhood, and by the time he is an adult he has a self-centered view of the world in which he believes that he is entitled to whatever he wants. Constantly he is sizing up his prospects for exploiting people and situations. To him the world is a chessboard, with other people serving as pawns to gratify his desires. This view of life is not only expressed in his actions but also pervades his fantasies.[41a]

> Playing the psychiatric game is exciting. Just like a crime, it offers a criminal opportunity to outsmart the system and make fools of everyone .... Because he is considered sick, his crimes of the past and violations of the present

are treated therapeutically, not punitively. This means to him that he will be able to get away with a lot more than he ever could in prison. He figures, often correctly, that he can do as he pleases as long as he shows remorse and psychological insight later. If he assaults another patient, he can talk about his pent-up hostility. If he uses illicit drugs, he can explain it as his seeking relief from overwhelming anxiety. If he tries to escape, he can relate it to intense depression. Sometimes he gets away with such psychological rationalizations and may even be praised for them.[42]

We are as we think. It is impossible to help a person give up crime and live responsibly without helping him to change what is most basic — his thinking. Criminals have been rewarded, punished, manipulated, probed for unconscious dynamics, and taught to read, work, and socialize, but they have not been helped to learn brand-new thinking patterns in order to change their way of life.[43]

According to Dr. Samenow, the criminal typically has an infantile personality, completely centered upon the needs, wants and desires of the self. What he desires, he seizes. What he covets, he takes. When he experiences feelings of rage, frustration, or dominance, he does not scruple to employ violence in expressing those feelings. In all these things, he tends to love and to admire the way he behaves, and to fault others for getting in his way. A human being who is not as moral as he or she ought to be at a given age is said to be immoral. The criminal is an underdeveloped moral being.

In summary, those who seek to avoid criminal acts must (1) restrain certain of their impulses. They must (2) respect others as ends, not solely as means. They must (3) cut through self-deception about their own purposes, views of reality, and weaknesses. Conversely, habitual criminals do the reverse: they do not restrain (they may even nurture) those of their impulses that lead to criminal acts; they treat other persons as means, not ends; and they are enmeshed in massive rationalizations and self-justifications, which allow them to maintain that their own way of thinking and acting is defensible. From such defects of virtue, criminal acts spring. Further, such defects prevent criminals from exercising their liberty as human persons. A person who gives way to criminal impulses, without self-restraint, is a slave of those impulses. He cannot "break the habit." He can hardly be expected to avoid future criminal acts. A person who does not treat others as ends is not free to enter into civilized conduct with other persons. A person who is dishonest about the implications of his own purposes, his view of reality, and his weaknesses is a victim of parts of his own inner life for which he is responsible. Quite dramatically, such a person is less than free. Habitual criminal conduct, therefore, follows from persistent personal failures to attain the full measure of human liberty. By contrast, in order to exercise genuine human liberty, a human being must form in himself a good character, with a full and appropriate set of moral skills.

7. TOWARD A CULTURE OF
MORAL DEVELOPMENT

Every human being is responsible for his own moral development. Still, moral development is, in part, a social task. It is much easier for individuals to assume responsibility for their own level of moral development when they live within a culture that nourishes such levels of moral development. On a visit to Iceland, some years ago, for example, I was told often of the extraordinarily low level of crime upon that lovely island. There had been one murder committed there many years ago, but none since, one journalist told me; "and that one was by a stranger." Indeed, in many localities in nearly all nations, there are communities in which violent crime is very low. Across nations and across time, variations in crime rates are quite remarkable. It is not for a philosopher to present a statistical portrait of such matters.[44] In keeping with the theme of this paper, I would like to concentrate by way of conclusion on several of the steps that might be taken within the culture of the United States to reduce the frequency of criminal behavior — or, more exactly, to increase the frequency of virtuous behavior. To focus on the more creative rather than on the more defensive task seems to me the more fruitful course.

It must be admitted that the teaching of virtue is not easy. Much more is required than learning *about* virtue. Virtue is *doing*. Virtue is acting well; it is learned through practice; it is the development of capacities for perception and insight, purpose and manner, swiftness in decision and exactness in execution.[45] Since every individual person is unique, and since circumstances and occasion are virtually infinite, virtue requires both a great deal of accurate self-knowledge and good, swift and true judgment concerning other persons and occasions.[46] It is more like an acquired habit than like the memorization of rules. It is more like an acquired art than like an ability to reason. For this reason, in describing virtue, Aristotle turned regularly to examples from athletics and from art.[47] Consider baseball: the technique that works for one batter may not work for another. A good batting coach is not an enforcer of rules. His task is to observe each hitter in his own strengths and weaknesses, instincts and skills, tendencies and abilites, in order to help each hitter to find the style most suitable to *him*. Virtuous acts, since they spring from a person inside-out, each carry a personal signature. For two different persons, virtuous action in the same situation might well require two different ways of acting.

There are, here as elsewhere in human life, materials of craft and lore that one person can pass on to another, as master to apprentice. Not only the young, all of us, in the progressively different situations we meet in life, learn best from observing closely those whom we judge to be the best performers. We learn, too, some "rules of thumb."

"Lean against one's prevailing tendencies," is one such.[48] Those who tend to be hesitant or timid need to learn to accept the risks of acting more quickly, before opportunity passes and regrets accumulate. Those who tend to be enthusiastic need to learn to pause, to reflect, and to exercise self-criticism — before they act.

Above all, then, virtue is learned in social contexts. We learn how to improve our moral skills from others. We are encouraged — or ridiculed — by others. If in American society as a whole we wish again to make every criminal "an enemy of the human race," we need also again to praise every man and woman of virtue as our friend.

Several obstacles stand in the way. First, our high culture — composed of intellectuals, professors, and artists — is quite ambivalent about praise for virtue and for character, as it is also ambivalent about strengthening the family. For many, such realities smack of "traditional values"' i.e., those residues of the dark past that "enlightenment" is supposed to "enlighten" us *from*.

Second, our academic tradition in the study of ethics has largely ignored the concepts of virtue and character. Neither the utilitarian tradition derived from Bentham nor the deontological tradition derived from Kant, neither the "pessimistic" image of human nature sketched in Hobbes nor the "romantic" image sketched in Rousseau, offers illumination about virtue and character. While the Aristotelian tradition is kept alive in Great Britain, and rather less so in the United States (outside the

Catholic intellectual tradition, at least), it seldom counts for a great deal in contemporary ethical discussion and its concepts are almost never clearly grasped or accurately presented. If one were to ask American intellectuals to define "virtue" and "character," there is reason to doubt, first, whether discussions of significant clarity would be forthcoming; or, second, whether the powerful arguments of the past would be known well enough to be embodied within them. Instead, amid allusions to the "Victorian Age" and to "bourgeois morality," it is often suggested that virtue and character connote a straitlaced, stiff, hypocritical, and conservative moral posture, from which "liberalism" or "progressivism" intend to "liberate" us.

These are serious intellectual errors of distortion and omission. Their consequences are also serious, because if clear concepts of virtue and character are not available at the highest intellectual level, it is not likely that they will be taken seriously in textbooks, curricula, and informed public discussion, even if they were there to be found, as, typically, they now are not.

Third, the needs of the entertainment media to some extent fly in the face of virtue and character, and to some extent totally depend upon them. The essential dependence of the media upon virtue and character follows from the inherent demands of the art of storytelling. Without character, "characters" would lack intelligibility; without virtue, they could not be attractive. Courage, kindness, tenderness, persistence, integrity, loyalty, and other virtues are indispensable to the storyteller's art. On the other hand, knowing well the burdens imposed upon them by virtue, audiences necessarily love plots in which heroes and heroines are tempted, fall, flout conventions, "kick against the goad," and in other ways rebel — at least against excessively conventional ways of understanding virtue and character.

In a profound sense, such real-life battles deepen our understanding of true virtue, true character, and — one almost wishes to add — "true grit." In a superficial sense, however, popular entertainment often depends on "shock value" and titillation. Its producers are always tempted to violate ethical norms just enough to offer a taste of "forbidden fruit," yet without creating too high a sense of alarm. When this is done cheaply and in tawdry fashion — through unnecessary nudity, sexual suggestion, violent behavior, and impulse-gratification — critics properly attack such products both on aesthetic and on moral grounds. Their work sometimes described as a moral "wasteland," producers of television shows and popular films at times seem to want it both ways: both to pay conventional respect to traditional values and to pander. It is plausible that ratings systems reward such compromises. Hungers for greater depth in programming often go unfulfilled.

In particular, given the pronounced religiousness of the American people — in belief and in practice, according to Gallup, among the most religious people in the world[49] — there is in the mass media a striking absence of significant drama about the struggles for virtue and character in America's plural religious traditions. Ordinarily, persons do not learn "virtue in general," rather, through their families and religious traditions, they learn the particular paths to virtue taught somewhat distinctively within each religious body. Some religious bodies are quite impulsive, for example, placing great stress on vivid emotional experiences in moments of conversion ("I accepted Jesus on May 27, 1972," one such communicant may recall). Others have more sober, restrained traditions that appeal much less to subjective experience and far more to objective disciplines and rites. Virtue, in the concrete, is typically communicated through particular communities of understanding, of method, and of style.

About many such matters, our intellectual and academic elites are remarkably incurious, and our national communications media have been (at least until recent years) remarkably reticent. By contrast, most seem eager to explore "new" moralities, fresh "liberations," new imperatives of "consciousness-raising," and the ongoing saga of "progressive" attitudes. The bias is pronounced. It exacts several social costs.

One such cost appears to be a gap between the cultures of academic and intellectual elites and those of the ordinary public. Another seems to be the vacuum created by the separation of the three major sub-systems (political, economic and moral-cultural) of our political economy.[50] This point needs some explication.

While explicit about the Republic's dependence upon the virtue and religiousness of its citizens, the Founders did not assign to government the task of "soulcraft." This it left to the leaders of the nation's moral and cultural institutions: principally to families, of course, and local communities, but also to the churches, the press (today, the "media"), and the universities and schools. For generations, the primary task explicitly assigned to the public schools of the nation was character formation.[51] McGuffey's readers exemplify the methods employed in teaching reading, writing and arithmetic; one learned from them, not only techniques, but classic statements of American purpose and American (Northern Protestant) virtue.[52]

In recent decades, by contrast, the teaching of virtue and character has explicitly *not* been the primary function of the public schools. Further, the mainline churches seem nowadays less to emphasize their long traditions of instruction in virtue and character, and more to emphasize counseling, therapeutic methods, and social causes. In the university world, emphasis upon virtue and character — such as Thomas Jefferson insisted upon in the schools of Virginia and at the University of Virginia[53] — would now seem to many not only quaint but perhaps threatening and even impermissible. Thus, at present, no major institution in this Republic appears to concern itself with the state of virtue and character; virtue and character have been orphaned.

Understandably, then, families concerned to instruct their children in virtue and character feel isolated and alone, when not under assault, even from the glowing screen in their own living rooms, and not infrequently even in church.

All this is not to say that the future is bleak. On the contrary, the American family and local communities have shown themselves to be amazingly resilient and persistent in continuing to instruct their youngsters in the classic paths of virtue and of character. In some ways, such institutions of immediate culture may prove to be far more powerful than the more remote cultures represented through larger institutions. There are significant indications, indeed, that a quiet moral revolution is underway, affecting not only communications elites but, in particular, some of the more influential intellectual and academic elites.

8. CONCLUDING REFLECTIONS

It was my good fortune, before this essay had been completed, that the magisterial book by James Q. Wilson and Richard J. Herrnstein, *Crime and Human Nature*, issued from the press, in time to help me anchor my reflections in a theory of human nature otherwise little accessible in social science. Observing that certain classic serious crimes appear in all cultures and in all historical periods, and that certain generalizations about criminal acts (e.g., that most crime is committed by young urban males) appear to be universally valid, Wilson and

Herrnstein link crime to human nature, while giving the latter concept scientific grounding. More than that, their researches lead them toward what they themselves do not scruple to call an Aristotelian approach. Even more exactly to the point, in their concluding chapter they introduce explicitly the useful concepts of virtue and character. Their way of reasoning and their conclusions considerably lifted my sagging sails.

Thinking in an Aristotelian way has long been my native intellectual habit. If there is one book in moral philosophy I cherish more than Aristotle's *Nicomachean Ethics*, it is the Commentary upon it by St. Thomas Aquinas — the first student in Western history to have Aristotle's text before his eyes since its disappearance a thousand years earlier, and after its discovery and translation into Latin.

Since the human mind often comes to understand one subject by contrast with its contraries, it has long seemed to me that one might come to understand crime through a study of virtue, and vice versa. In both, human will and settled dispositions, inherited temperament and socially acquired habits seem to play prominent roles. Moreover, my studies of Anglo-American ethics at Harvard during the 1960s had left me unsatisfied with the current state of ethical reflection, in which virtue barely figures if at all, a dissatisfaction brilliantly articulated recently by Alasdair MacIntyre in *After Virtue*.[54] Meanwhile basic concepts of virtue and character have begun to appear in the work of leading Protestant ethicists, such as James Gustufson[55] and Stanley Hauerwas.[56] Finally, in "A Thanksgiving Day Statement" in 1984, several prominent educators issued a manifesto for the public schools, *Developing Character: Transmitting Knowledge*.[57]

Thus, it seems, considerable intellectual movement is afoot. In the population at large, there are also signs of renewed moral seriousness. The task now is to establish the latter on a sound intellectual basis, so that it may permanently enter the consciousness of our culture in articulate and self-critical ways, both in high culture and in popular culture.

To summarize, then, the main points of my thesis. One of the contraries of crime is virtue. Rather than inquiring into the causes of crime, it seems useful to inquire into the causes of virtue, particularly its cultural causes. Although highly praised as crucial social realities during most of the history of the American Republic, virtue and character have fallen into public neglect. The *ethos* of our culture shifted, rather suddenly, from one of self-control to one of impulse-release. Meanwhile, habitual criminals appear from abundant evidence to be persons who exhibit significant defects of virtue: in failing to restrain certain destructive impulses; in treating other persons as means, not as ends; and in self-deception. Major American institutions — the academy, the schools, the popular entertainments of the media, and even the churches — have disparaged or forgotten the principles of virtue and character. Yet an *ethos* that has changed in one direction may, at least in principle, be altered by human effort so as to swing in another. In particular, if a life of habitual crime is understood to spring from a willing defect of virtue, then those who choose such a life must be confronted with its full moral and social implications, and encouraged to shoulder those human responsibilities which are the source of human dignity.

From such propositions, several testable hypotheses emerge:

(1) Can a program aimed at treating criminals as persons, as ends, that is, as responsible, originating causes of their own acts, help them to rise up from the level of impulse-gratification to the level of ethical reflection, so that they take responsibility for their own habits and actions? The results reported by Dr. Samenow suggest that in some cases it can.[58]

(2) Can a program in public schools in high crime areas, aimed at character formation and at practice in the virtues, show significant results in the behavior of young adults?

(3) Can a community-based program of concerned parents in high-crime areas, to the same ends, show significant results?

(4) In many poor, high-crime, high-unemployment areas, there is no shortage of work to be done (glazing windows, painting, carpentry, plumbing); might an experimental program in teaching the related crafts and associated virtues of responsibility create sufficient rewards such as to

reduce both crime and unemployment? (There *are* poor neighborhoods in which industriousness is the norm, not the exception.)

(5) More generally, can an emphasis upon the *internal* causes of virtue and on the *internal* sources of high self-esteem rather than on the *external* circumstances in which young males in high-crime areas find themselves, alter the ethical horizons of such youngsters, so as to reduce the incidence of crime?

(6) On a larger scale, could a change in leading cultural institutions — the churches, the media, the universities, and public discourse in general — in the direction of emphasizing character-formation and both personal and civic virtue, praising socially responsible actions and ridiculing socially destructive actions, result in a change of *ethos* so powerful as eventually and significantly to reduce the incidence of crime? Such a mammoth undertaking might be years in the launching. Its fruits might not be measurable except in very long time-frames. Yet there is historical evidence both that the *ethos* of a culture is subject to change, and that such changes seem to have some effect upon the practice of virtue and the shaping of character, and thus upon the incidence of criminal behavior.

After so long an essay, then, a summarizing word: The roots of crime, dear reader, lie not in our stars, but in ourselves. In the words of William James:

> The solving word, for the learned and the unlearned man alike, lies in the last resort in

the dumb willingnesses and unwillingnesses of their interior characters, and nowhere else. It is not in heaven, neither is it beyond the sea; but the word is very nigh unto thee, in thy mouth and in thy heart, that thou mayest do it.[59]

NOTES

1. "Political oeconomy, considered as a branch of the science of a statesman or legislator, proposes two distinct objects; first, to provide a plentiful revenue or subsistence for the people, or more properly to enable them to provide such a revenue or subsistence for themselves; and secondly, to supply the state or commonwealth with a revenue sufficient for the publick services. It proposes to enrich both the people and the sovereign." Adam Smith, *An Inquiry into the Nature and Causes of the Wealth of Nations*, ed. R. H. Campbell and A. S. Skinner, 2 vols. (1776; reprint ed., Oxford University Press, 1979, Indianapolis, Indiana: Liberty Classics, 1981), Book IV, "Of Systems of political Oeconomy," 1:429. Gertrude Himmelfard adds: "For Smith political economy was not an end in itself but a means to an end, that end being the wealth and well-being, moral and material, of the 'people,' of whom the 'laboring poor' were the largest part." *The Idea of Poverty: England in the Early Industrial Age* (New York: Alfred A. Knopf, 1984), p. 63.

2. James Q. Wilson and Richard J. Herrnstein, *Crime and Human Nature* (New York: Simon Schuster, 1985), p. 137. The figure "about six percent" comes from one study in Wisconsin; I cite it as indicative of a range. See also pp. 21, 26 ff., and the whole of Chapter 5, "Age."

3. Aristotle's concept of virtue is subtle. His discussion of virtue as a "mean" between two "extremes," commonly taught in the schools, is merely a heuristic device that did not work out; he himself went beyond it. The following texts from the *Nicomachean Ethics* suggest the complexity and richness of his insight:

> Hence while in respect of its substance and the definition that states what it really is in essence virtue is the observance of the mean, in point of excellence and rightness it is an extreme.   [II, vi, 17.]

... excellence or virtue in a man will be the disposition which renders him a good man and also which will cause him to perform his function well.   [II, vi, 3.]

[Thus, man's happiness, his supreme good, is] the end of political science, but the principal care of this science is to produce a certain character in the citizens, namely to make them virtuous, and capable of performing noble actions.   [I, ix, 8.]

Virtue then is a settled disposition of the mind determining the choice of actions and emotions, consisting essentially in the observance of the mean relative to us, this being determined by principle, that is, as the prudent man would determine it.   [II, vi, 15.]

For the good man judges everything correctly; what things truly are, that they seem to him to be ... what chiefly distinguishes the good man is that he sees the truth in each kind, being himself as it were the standard and measure of the noble and pleasant.   [III, iv, 4-5.]

... everyone, even at the present day, in defining Virtue, after saying what disposition it is and specifying the things with which it is concerned, adds that it is a disposition determined by the right principle; and the right principle is the principle determined by Prudence.... This formula however requires a slight modification. Virtue is not merely a disposition conforming to right principle, but one co-operating with right principle; and Prudence is right principle in matters of conduct.   [VI, xiii, 4-5.]

... men are themselves responsible for having become careless through living carelessly, as they are for being unjust or profligate if they do wrong or pass their time in drinking and dissipation. They acquire a particular quality by constantly acting in a particular way. This is shown by the way in which men train themselves for some contest or pursuit: they practice continually. Therefore only an utterly senseless person can fail to know that our characters are the result of our conduct; but if a man knowingly acts in a way that will result in his becoming unjust, he must be said to be voluntarily unjust.   [III, v, 10-12.]

Natural endowment is obviously not under our control; it is bestowed on those who are fortunate, in the true sense, by some divine dispensation. Again, theory and teaching are not, I fear, equally efficacious in all cases: the soil must have been previously tilled if it is to foster the seed, the mind of the pupil must have been prepared by the cultivation of habits, so as to like and dislike aright .... We must therefore by some means secure that the *character* shall have at the outset a natural affinity for virtue, loving what is noble and hating what is base. And it is difficult to obtain a right education in virtue from youth up without being brought up under right laws; for to live temperately and hardily is not pleasant to most men, especially when young....   [X, ix, 6-8; emphasis added.]

The best thing is then that there should be a proper system of public regulation; but when the matter is neglected by the community, it would seem to be the duty of the individual to assist his own children and friends to attain virtue, or even if not able to do so successfully, at all events to make this his aim.   [X, ix, 14.]

4. Ibid., X, ix, 5.

5. ... it makes a great difference whether we conceive the Supreme Good to depend on possessing virtue or on displaying it — on disposition, or on the manifestation of a disposition in action. For a man may possess the disposition without its producing any good result, as for instance when he is asleep, or has ceased to function from some other cause; but virtue in active exercise cannot be

117

inoperative — it will of necessity act, and act well. And just as at the Olympic games the wreaths of victory are not bestowed upon the handsomest and strongest persons present, but on men who enter for the competitions ... so it is those who act rightly who carry off the prizes and good things of life.   [Ibid., I, viii, 9.]

... a man becomes just by doing just actions and temperate by doing temperate actions; and no one can have the remotest chance of becoming good without doing them. But the mass of mankind, instead of doing virtuous acts, have recourse to discussing virtue, and fancy that they are pursuing philosophy and that this will make them good men ....   [Ibid., II, iv, 5-6.]

6. ... while great and frequent reverses can crush and mar our bliss both by the pain they cause and by the hindrance they offer to many activities. Yet nevertheless even in adversity nobility shines through, when a man endures repeated and severe misfortune with patience, not owing to insensibility but from generosity and greatness of soul ... no supremely happy man can ever become miserable. For he will never do hateful or base actions, since we hold that the truly good and wise man will bear all kinds of fortune in a seemly way, and will always act in the noblest manner that the circumstances allow ....   [Ibid., I, x, 12-13.]

7. But if happiness consists in activity in accordance with virtue, it is reasonable that it should be activity in accordance with the highest virtue; and this will be the virtue of the best part of us ... it is the activity of this part of us in accordance with the virtue proper to it that will constitute perfect happiness; and ... this activity is the activity of contemplation."   [Ibid., X, vii, 1.]

... activity in accordance with wisdom is admittedly the most pleasant of the activities in accordance with virtue:

at all events it is held that philosophy or the pursuit of wisdom contains pleasures of marvellous purity and permanence, and it is reasonable to suppose that the enjoyment of knowledge is a still pleasanter occupation than the pursuit of it. [Ibid., X, vii, 3.]

[A contemplative life] ... will be higher than the human level: not in virtue of his humanity will a man achieve it, but in virtue of something within him that is divine; and by as much as this something is superior to his composite nature, by so much is its activity superior to the exercise of the other forms of virtue. If then the intellect is something divine in comparison with man, so is the life of the intellect divine in comparison with human life. [Ibid., X, vii, 8.]

Nor ought we to obey those who enjoin that a man should have man's thoughts and a mortal the thoughts of mortality, but we ought so far as possible to achieve immortality, and do all that man may to live in accordance with the highest thing in him; for though this be small in bulk, in power and value it far surpasses all the rest. [Ibid., X, vii, 8.]

... the activity of God, which is transcendent in blessedness, is the activity of contemplation; and therefore among human activities that which is most akin to the divine activity of contemplation will be the greatest source of happiness. [Ibid., X, viii, 7.]

8. Experience forced Stanton E. Samenow and his colleague, Samuel Yochelson, to change their approach to the causes of crime: "Criminals *choose* to commit crimes. Crime resides within the person and is 'caused' by the way he thinks, not by his environment. Criminals think differently from responsible people. What must change is how the offender views himself and the world. Focusing on forces outside the criminal is futile. We found the conventional psychological

and sociological formulations about crime and its causes to be erroneous and counterproductive because they provide excuses. In short, we did a 180-degree turn in our thinking about crime and its causes. From regarding criminals as victims we saw that instead they were victimizers who had freely chosen their way of life." *Inside the Criminal Mind* (New York: Times Books, 1984), p. xiv; emphasis added.

9. "There is absolutely nothing new in the pragmatic method. Socrates was an adept at it. Aristotle used it methodically. Locke, Berkeley, and Hume made momentous contributions to truth by its means .... But these forerunners used it in fragments: they were preludes only. Not until in our time has it generalized itself, become conscious of a universal mission, pretended to a conquering destiny. I believe in that destiny, and I hope I may end by inspiring you with my belief." William James, "Pragmatism," in *Pragmatism and Other Essays* (New York: Washington Square Press, 1963), p. 25. An essay of mine on this tradition, "The Traditional Pragmatism," appeared in *The Journal of Ecumenical Studies* (1967), and was reprinted with commentary in Michael Novak, *A Time to Build* (New York: Macmillan, 1967), pp. 321-353. In metaphysics, James departed from the Great Tradition in key respects, but in ethics he wished to renew it in his own distinctive way.

10. Frederick A. Hayek places himself in the "Whig" tradition of practical wisdom and cites Aquinas as a forebear: "... in some respects Lord Acton was not being altogether paradoxical when he described Thomas Aquinas as the first Whig." *The Constitution of Liberty* (Chicago: Henry Regnery, 1960), p. 457, n. 4.

11. As James Q. Wilson and Richard J. Hernnstein have written: "Modern criminology has by and large taken one of two views of human nature. The first [**Hobbesian one**] is that man is a self-seeking rational calculator who responds to the rewards and punishments he encounters in his dealings with

others. The second [**Rousseauean one**] is that man is naturally good; his goodness will be realized if social arrangements are decent, corrupted if they are defective." *Crime and Human Nature*, p. 514. See the whole of Chapter 20, "Human Nature and the Political Order."

12. Pastoral Letter Issued by the Third Plenary Council of Baltimore, 7 December 1884, in Hugh J. Nolan, ed., *Pastoral Letters of the United States Catholic Bishops*, 4 vols. (Washington, D.C.: United States Catholic Conference, 1984), 1:228.

13. "**P**rudent political thinkers have more worries than appear prominently in Madison's philosophy. The American Founders talked almost exclusively about institutional arrangements and the sociology of factions presupposed by the institutional arrangements. They talked little about the sociology of virtue, or the husbandry of exemplary elites ...." George Will, *Statecraft as Soulcraft: What Government Does* (New York: Simon and Schuster, 1983), p. 40.

14. In some ways, modern society demands *more* virtue of citizens than earlier societies: the virtues proper to democracy and to economic development, for example, as well as acceptance of the disciplines of time and schedules, the self-denial implicit in new knowledge concerning health care, and the rest. While mocking the vices and follies of our age, one must also note the plusses on the balance sheet.

15. "In a genuinely pluralistic society, there is no one sacred canopy. *By intention* there is not. At its spiritual core, there is an empty shrine. That shrine is left empty in the knowledge that no one word, image, or symbol is worthy of what all seek there. Its emptiness, therefore represents the transcendence which is approached by free consciences from a virtually infinite number of directions." Michael Novak, *The Spirit of Democratic Capitalism* (New York: Simon and Schuster, 1982), p. 53; emphasis in original. See also James

NOTES

Nuechterlein, "A Sacred Canopy," review of *The Naked Public Square*, by Richard John Neuhaus, in *Commentary*, January 1985, pp. 78-80.

16. Richard John Neuhaus, *The Naked Public Square: Religion and Democracy in America* (Grand Rapids, Michigan: Eerdmans, 1984).

17. "The specifying note of political association is its rational deliberative quality, its dependence for its permanent cohesiveness on argument among men. In this it differs from all other forms of association found on earth." John Courtney Murray, S.J., *We Hold These Truths* (New York: Sheed and Ward, 1960), p. 6. Murray also quotes from Thomas Gilby, O.P., *Between Community and Society* (New York: Longmans, Green & Co., 1953): " 'Civilization is formed by men locked together in argument. From this dialogue the community becomes a political community' " (ibid.). Jacques Maritain reiterates the point: "Justice is a primary condition for the existence of the body politic, but Friendship is its very life-giving form." *Man and the State* (Chicago: University of Chicago Press, 1951), p. 10.

18. See Wilson and Hernnstein, *Crime and Human Nature*, Part II, "Constitutional Factors."

19. See the Federal Bureau of Investigation's annual *Uniform Crime Reports for the United States*, (Washington, D.C.: U.S. Government Printing Office, 1929-).

20. James Q. Wilson, "Crime and American Culture," *The Public Interest*, Winter 1983, pp. 22-48. Reprinted above as Introduction. See also Chapter 16, "Historical Trends in Crime," in Wilson and Herrnstein, *Crime and Human Nature*, pp. 407-438.

21. See Perry Miller, *Errand into the Wilderness*, (Cambridge: Harvard University Press, 1956). Wilson, in "Crime

and American Culture," adds that "On the eve of the Revolutionary War, many colonists — and not only Tories — feared that if rebellion came, 'the bands of society would be dissolved, the harmony of the world confounded, and the order of nature subverted' .... This did not happen — not, at least, during or after the war .... The small towns and villages of which the infant republic was composed seemed quite able, by using public opinion to enforce a communal consensus, to maintain an orderly society."

22. Ibid., p. 22.

23. Maritain distinguished sharply between the state and society. He hoped that "... the State would leave to the multifarious organs of the social body the autonomous initiative and management of all the activities which by nature pertain to them. Its only prerogative in this respect would be its genuine prerogative as topmost umpire and supervisor, regulating those spontaneous and autonomous activities from the superior political point of view of the common good.

"So perhaps it will be possible ... to make the State into a topmost agency concerned only with the final supervision of the achievements of institutions born out of freedom, whose free interplay expressed the vitality of a society integrally just in its basic structure." Jacques Maritain, *Man and the State*, p. 23. The precise distinction between the state and society is made earlier: "The *Body Politic* or the *Political Society* is the whole. The *State* is a part — the topmost part — of this whole" (p. 10). "The State is only that part of the body politic especially concerned with the maintenance of law, the promotion of the common welfare and public order, and the administration of public affairs. The State is a part which *specializes* in the interests of the *whole*" (p. 11). "The State is inferior to the body politic as a whole. Is the State even the *head* of the body politic? Hardly, for in the human being the head is an instrument of such spiritual powers as the intellect and will, which the whole body has to serve; whereas the

NOTES

functions exercised by the State are for the body politic, and not the body politic for them" (p. 13).

24. Note, among others, three passages in Tocqueville: (1) "Better use has been made of association and this powerful instrument of action has been applied to more varied aims in America than anywhere else in the world." (2) "Americans of all ages, all stations of life, and all types of disposition are forever forming associations. There are not only commercial and industrial associations in which all take part, but others of a thousand different types — religious, moral, serious, futile, very general and very limited, immensely large and very minute. Americans combine to give fetes, found seminaries, build churches, distribute books, and send missionaries to the antipodes. Hospitals, prisons and schools take shape in that way. Finally, if they want to proclaim a truth or propagate some feeling by the encouragement of a great example, they form an association." (3) "Among laws controlling human societies there is one more precise and clearer, it seems to me, than all the others. If men are to remain civilized or to become civilized, the art of association must develop and improve among them at the same speed as equality of conditions spreads." Alexis de Tocqueville, *Democracy in America*, ed. J. P. Mayer, trans. George Lawrence (New York: Doubleday and Co., 1966), pp. 189, 513,517.

Recent students of Tocqueville reaffirm this point: "James Curtis, in 'Voluntary Associaton Joining: A Cross-National Comparative Note,' *American Sociological Review* 36 (1971): 872-80, finds that voluntary association membership in Canada and the United States is significantly higher than in Great Britain, Germany, Italy, and Mexico .... Sidney Verba, Norman H. Nie, and Jae-on Kim, in *Participation and Political Equality: A Seven Nation Comparison* (New York: Cambridge University Press, 1978), ... find Americans highest in active membership in 'organizations engaged in solving community problems' but relatively low in membership in political parties, clubs, and organizations .... Alex Inkeles in 'The American Character,' in *The Center Magazine*, a publica-

124

tion of the Center for the Study of Democratic Institutions, November/December, 1983, pp. 25-39, reports continuity in community involvement from Tocqueville's time to the present. He finds many other continuities, including self-reliance and a sense of individual efficacy." Robert N. Bellah, et al., *Habits of the Heart: Individualism and Commitment in American Life* (Berkeley, California: University of California Press, 1985), p. 321, n.1.

25. Tocqueville, *Democracy in America*, p. 96.

26. Lionel Trilling writes: "Between the end of the first quarter of this century and the present time there has grown up a populous group whose members take for granted the idea of an adversary culture. This group is to be described not only by its increasing size but by its increasing coherence. It is possible to think of it as a class." Moreover, "Any historian of the literature of the modern age will take virtually for granted the adversary intention, the actually subversive intention, that characterizes modern writing — he will perceive its clear purpose of detaching the reader from the habits of thought and feeling that the larger culture imposes, of giving him a ground and a vantage point from which to judge and condemn, and perhaps revise, the culture that produced him." Lionel Trilling, *Beyond Culture: Essays on Literature and Learning* (New York: Viking Press, 1968), pp. xiii and xii-xiii, respectively.

27. The literature on the "new class" is immense. See, for example, B. Bruce-Briggs, ed., *The New Class?* (New Brunswick, N.J.: Transaction Books, 1979). The concept was first employed by writers on the left: David T. Bazelon, *Power in America* (New York: New American Library, 1967); John Kenneth Galbraith, *The Affluent Society* (Boston: Houghton Mifflin, 1958), Chapter 14; Michael Harrington, *Toward a Democratic Left* (New York: Macmillan, 1968), Chapter 10. See also my "Needing Niebuhr Again," *Commentary*, September 1972, pp. 52-60.

28. My own experience as a speechwriter in congressional and presidential campaigns in 1970, 1972, and 1976 illuminated this tacit but effective prohibition quite powerfully. Local urban politicians invariably stressed the crime issue; national Democratic politicians feared it.

29. See Daniel Yankelovich, *The Changing Values on Campus* (New York: Washington Square Press, 1972); *The New Morality: A Profile of America Youth in the Seventies* (New York: McGraw Hill, 1974). Yankelovich discusses how the changing *ethos* has evolved to the present in *New Rules: Searching for Self-Fulfillment in a World Turned Upside Down* (New York: Random House, 1981).

30. At the experimental college of the SUNY system, Old Westbury, several of us, in defiance of the prevailing cult of openness and impulse-expression, founded the so-designated Disciplines College. See Michael Novak, "The Disciplines Curriculum at Old Westbury," *Soundings*, Summer 1969.

31. See William Ryan, *Blaming the Victim* (New York: Random House, 1972).

32. "... the *in*visible one today, surely, is not the jobless youth of the streets, or even the welfare mother, but the successful middle-class black with the stable family and ascendent career. He is rapidly becoming the majority of his race in this country. But as he succeeds, he is explained away ...." George Gilder, *Visible Man: A True Story of Post-racist America* (New York: Basic Books, 1978), p. x; emphasis in original.

33. See Wilson and Herrnstein, *Crime and Human Nature*, Chapter 18, "Race and Crime."

34. Wilson, "Crime and American Culture," p. 30.

35. Ibid., p. 35.

36. Happiness or, in other words, "the Good of man is the active exercise of his soul's faculties in conformity with excellence or virtue .... Moreover this activity must occupy a complete lifetime; for one swallow does not make spring, nor does one fine day; and similarly one day or a brief period of happiness does not make a man supremely blessed and happy." *Nicomachean Ethics*, I, vii, 15-16.

37. "As the sciences of behavior evolve, it will become more and more apparent how tied human actions are to the circumstance in which they occur, but the legal system will continue to need to determine whether an offense deserves punishment. The confrontation between science and the criterion of free action has already distorted and inhibited the operation of the criminal justice system .... As scientific knowledge grows, the distortions and inhibitions will worsen, unless the criterion is dropped, replaced by a conception that preserves personal responsibility without denying, perhaps even making practical use of, the growing knowledge about the sources of criminal behavior." Wilson and Herrnstein, *Crime and Human Nature*, p. 507.

38. The best treatment I have found is in St. Thomas Aquinas, *Summa Contra Gentiles*, Book III, and the best exposition of its fundamental concepts, Bernard Lonergan, S.J., *Grace and Freedom: Operative Grace in the Thought of St. Thomas Aquinas*, ed. J. Patout Burns, S.J., with an Introduction by Frederick E. Crowe, S.J. (London: Darton, Longman and Todd and New York: Herder and Herder, 1971).

39. "Millions of items of the outward order are present to my senses which never properly enter into my experience. Why? Because they have no *interest* for me. *My experience is what I agree to attend to.* Only those items which I *notice* shape my mind — without selective interest, experience is an utter chaos. Interest alone gives accent and emphasis, light and shade, background and foreground — intelligible perspective, in a word." William James, *The Principles of Psychology*,

2 vols. (New York: Henry Holt & Co., 1890), 1:402; emphasis in original.

40. "... our moral dispositions are formed as a result of the corresponding activities. Hence it is incumbent on us to control the character of our activities, since on the quality of these depends the quality of our dispositions. It is therefore not of small moment whether we are trained from childhood in one set of habits or another; on the contrary, it is of very great, or rather of supreme, importance." *Nicomachean Ethics*, II, i, 7-8.

41. Jacques Maritain, *Man and the State*, p. 13. Maritain is obviously playing on Mark 2:27: "The sabbath was made for man, not man for the sabbath."

41a. Samenow, *Inside the Criminal Mind*, p. 95.

42. Ibid., pp. 134-135.

43. Ibid., p. 257.

44. On this and other matters, Wilson and Herrnstein's *Crime and Human Nature* is a useful compendium of information.

45. Nor is prudence a knowledge of general principles only: it must take account of particular facts, since it is concerned with action, and action deals with particular things. This is why men who are ignorant of general principles are sometimes more successful in action than others who know them ... [often] men of experience are more successful than theorists. [*Nicomachean Ethics*, VI, vii, 7.]

Consequently the unproved assertions and opinions of experienced and elderly people, or of prudent men, are as much deserving of attention as those which they support by proof; for experience has given them an eye for things, and so they see correctly.   [Ibid., VI, xi, 6.]

... it is by the practical experience of life and conduct that the truth is really tested, since it is there that the final decision lies.   [Ibid., X, viii, 12.]

... in the practical sciences the end is not to attain a theoretic knowledge of the various subjects, but rather to carry out our theories in action. If so, to know what virtue is is not enough; we must endeavor to possess and to practice it, or in some other manner actually ourselves to become good.   [Ibid., X, viii, 1-2.]

... the end of this science [of prudence or practical wisdom] is not knowledge but action.   [ibid., I, iii, 6.]

... our present study [of prudence or practical wisdom], unlike the other branches of philosophy, has a practical aim (for we are not investigating the nature of virtue for the sake of knowing what it is, but in order that we may become good, without which result our investigation would be of no use) ....   [Ibid., II, ii, 1.]

... matters of conduct and expediency have nothing fixed or invariable about them, any more than have matters of health. And if this is true of the general theory of ethics, still less is exact precision possible in dealing with particular cases of conduct; for these come under no science of professional tradition, but the agents themselves have to consider what is suited to the circumstances on each occasion, just as is the case with the art of medicine or of navigation.   [Ibid., II, ii, 3-4.]

46. ... the whole theory of conduct is bound to be an outline only and not an exact system .... Matters of conduct and expediency have nothing fixed or invariable

about them, any more than have matters of health. And if this is true of the general theory of ethics, still less is exact precision possible in dealing with particular cases of conduct; for these come under no science or professional tradition, but the agents themselves have to consider what is suited to the circumstances on each occasion, just as is the case with the art of medicine or of navigation. [Ibid., II, ii, 3-4.]

... individual treatment is better than a common system, in education as in medicine. As a general rule rest and fasting are good for a fever, but they may not be best for a particular case; and presumably a professor of boxing does not impose the same style of fighting on all his pupils. It would appear then that private attention gives more accurate results in particular cases, for the particular subject is more likely to get the treatment that suits him. [Ibid., X, ix, 15.]

Yet to what degree and how seriously a man must err to be blamed is not easy to define on principle. For in fact no object of perception is easy to define; and such questions of degree depend on particular circumstances, and the decision lies with perception. [Ibid., II, ix, 8.]

... to feel these feelings at the right time, on the right occasion, towards the right people, for the right purpose and in the right manner, is to feel the best amount of them ... and the best amount of them is of course the mark of virtue. [Ibid., II, vi, 11.]

47. Again, the actions from or through which any virtue is produced are the same as those through which it also is destroyed — just as is the case with skill in the arts, for both the good harpers and the bad ones are produced by harping, and similarly with builders and all the other craftsmen: as you will become a good builder by building well, so you become a bad one from building badly. Were

this not so, there would be no need for teachers of the arts, but everybody would be born a good or bad craftsman as the case might be. [Ibid., II, i, 6-7.]

... pleasure causes us to do base actions and pain causes us to abstain from doing noble actions. Hence the importance, as Plato points out, of having been definitely trained from childhood to like and dislike the proper things; this is what good education means. [Ibid., II, iii, 2.]

... so it would appear that those who aspire to a scientific knowledge of politics require practical experience as well as study .... Nor ... is [it] easy to frame a constitution by making a collection of such existing laws as are reputed to be good ones, on the assumption that one can then select the best among them; as if even this selection did not call for understanding, and as if to judge correctly were not a very difficult task, just as much as it is for instance in music. It is only the experts in an art, who can judge correctly the productions of that art, and who understand the means and the method by which perfection is attained, and know which elements harmonize with which; amateurs may be content if they can discern whether the general result produced is good or bad, for example in the art of painting. Laws are the product, so to speak, of the art of politics; how then can a mere collection of laws teach a man the science of legislation, or make him able to judge which of them are the best? We do not see men becoming expert physicians from a study of medical handbooks. Yet medical writers attempt to describe not only general courses of treatment, but also methods of cure and modes of treatment for particular sorts of patients, classified according to their various habits of body; and their treatises appear to be of value for men who have had practical experience, though they are useless for the novice. [Ibid., X, ix, 20-21.]

NOTES

48. ... [The first practical rule] in aiming at the mean is to avoid that extreme which is the more opposed to the mean .... For of the two extremes one is a more serious error than the other. Hence, inasmuch as to hit the mean extremely well is difficult, the second best way to sail, as the saying goes, is to take the least of the evils ....   [Ibid., II, ix, 3-4.]

> The second rule is to notice what are the errors to which we are ourselves most prone (as different men are inclined by nature to different faults) ... then we must drag ourselves away in the opposite direction, for by steering wide of our besetting error we shall make a middle course. This is the method adopted by carpenters to straighten warped timber.   [Ibid., II, ix, 4-5.]

That the device of the "middle point" is heuristic, and not literal, becomes clear in passages such as this:

> ... it is such a mean because it aims at hitting the middle point in feelings and in actions .... [A]nybody can become angry ... give and spend money; but to be angry with or give money to the right person, and to the right amount, and at the right time, and for the right purpose, and in the right way — that is not within everybody's power and is not easy ....   [Ibid., II, ix, 1-2.]

49. See, for example, Gallup's international comparison of the frequency of prayer, reported in *Emerging Trends*, a publication of the Princeton Religious Research Center, March 1985. Each year the Princeton Religious Research Center also publishes *Religion in America*, a book-length report of the Gallup poll.

50. See Chapter 9, "Continuous Revolution," in my *Spirit of Democratic Capitalism*, pp. 171-186.

51. "The origins and aspirations of the public school move-

ment were thoroughly entwined with ... moralistic reform movements. From the beginning, the purpose of the tax-supported public school was character formation subordinate to 'the goal of character building,' even in programs that emphasized manual arts.'' Wilson and Hernnstein, *Crime and Human Nature*, p. 433.

52. See John Silber, Commencement Address to Boston University (Boston: Boston University, 1981). (Pamphlet.)

53. See Thomas Jefferson, "Report of the Commission for the University of Virginia (August 14, 1818)'', in *Thomas Jefferson* (New York: The Library of America, 1984), pp.457-75, esp. pp. 459-60.

54. Alasdair MacIntyre, *After Virtue: A Study in Moral Theory* (Notre Dame, Indiana: University of Notre Dame Press, 1981), especially Chapter 16, "From the Virtues to Virtue and After Virtue.''

55. See James Gustafson, *Christ and the Moral Life* (Chicago: University of Chicago Press, 1979); *Ethics from a Theocentric Perspective: Theology and Ethics*, 2 vols. (Chicago: University of Chicago Press, 1981, 1984).

56. See Stanley Hauerwas, *Vision and Virtue* (Notre Dame, Indiana: Fides, 1974); *Truthfulness and Tragedy* (Notre Dame, Indiana: University of Notre Dame Press, 1977); *Character and the Moral LIfe* (San Antonio, Texas: Trinity University Press, 1975).

57. See Edward A. Wynne, ed., *Developing Characters: Transmitting Knowledge: Sustaining the Momentum for Reform in American Education* (St. Posen, Illinois: The Thanksgiving Statement Group, 1984).

58. Samenow reports that the only meaningful statistics with respect to his and Yochelson's work occur during the

years 1970 to 1976 when their new habilitative procedures were used with 30 hard-core criminals. "As of May 1976, 13 out of 30 were living responsible lives .... These men not only were arrest-free, but they reported having very few desires to commit a crime. They were accountable for how they spent their money and time. Not only did they hold jobs, but they had developed stable work patterns and were advancing. Those who had families were described as accommodating and dependable. One could contend that the numbers are small, it is hard to generalize beyond them. On the other hand, 13 out of 30 represents better than a 33 percent success rate with men whom others had given up on. Each of the habilitated criminals had been a one-man crime wave." Samenow, *Inside the Criminal Mind*, pp. 250-251.

59. William James, "The Moral Philosopher and the Moral Life," in *Pragmatism and Other Essays*, p. 235.

Postscript

Reflections on 'Character and Crime'
by **Albert J. Reiss, Jr.** Yale University

At the outset, I also wish to demur. It is unclear whether I am qualified to discuss a treatise on crime and virtue by a philosopher. I am the product of an empirical training in the social sciences at the University of Chicago. Moreover, possessing an undergraduate degree in philosophy from a Jesuit institution, I am inclined to be disputatious and doubting in the pursuit of the truth.

Though exposed to many positivists at Chicago, I learned that while societies exist in and through concerted action, they are fundamentally normative. One of my professors used to remind us of this by reference to an ancient dialogue. When asked what holds the world up, the simple answer is, of course, Atlas. And upon inquiring as to what holds Atlas up, the answer is a turtle. To those refusing to regard this as a full answer and persist by asking what holds up the turtle, the final answer is values. Only the tenacious will seek an answer to the next question.

A problem for social scientists, and I suspect also for many philosophers, is that it is not a simple matter to reconcile rational with moral man and fact with belief. I recall vividly my own struggle upon learning in Applied Ethics that gambling was not per se immoral but that it was indeed immoral to bet on a sure thing. My rational self did not want to

135

give up the notion that a sure thing was the only bet a sensible person would make! The matter is resolved only when one sees that bet as deceit and believes deceit to be immoral.

Perhaps all of this is a prolegomenon to say that as a social scientist, I do not wish to be placed in either of Mr. Novak's social science traditions, neither that of Hobbes and its social science variants of strict behaviorism and utilitarianism nor Rousseau's social determinism. The pursuit of truth requires no such allegiance. But, I hasten to add, that I, like him, think that the relationship between moral character and misconduct sadly has been neglected in our attempts to understand crime and criminality.

POLAR WORDS IN DISCOURSE

St. Augustine once wrote — one can imagine somewhat in despair — "Oh, that the reality of things might overcome the tyranny of words!" A difficulty with words like vice and virtue is that they derive meaning primarily in terms of their opposites. The cardinal virtues of prudence, courage, temperance, and justice require their opposites as do the natural virtues of faith, hope, and charity. Another difficulty with words like *vice* and *virtue* is that each covers a diverse world of reality and often one's remarks are directed at only a part of that reality, such as crime and law-abidingness. Because words like vice and virtue can be seen primarily in terms of their opposites, it is all too easy to slip into thinking that those who do not commit common crimes are virtuous while those who do, are not. Yet, we know that is often far from the case. There are, for example, virtuous people called white-collar criminals and one need not imagine a Robin Hood to recognize that many so-called common criminals are not altogether lacking in virtues.

Thurman Arnold called words that can be used meaningfully only in relation to their opposites, polar words. Vice and virtue, criminal and non-criminal, law-abiding and law violating, just and unjust are polar words. He warned that they set traps for us:

> A reformer who wants to abolish injustice and create a world in which nothing but justice prevails is like a man who wants to make everything "up". Such a man might feel that if he took the lowest in the world and carried it to the highest point and kept on doing this, everything would eventually become "up".

But, he observed:

> This would certainly move a great many objects and create an enormous amount of activity. It might or might not be useful, according to the standards which we apply. However it would never result in the abolition of "down."

He then went on to say: "In the continuing debate over crime, for example, those who believe that the courts have become too lenient are heard to say: 'We must show more concern for the victim and less for the criminal.' To which another group retorts that 'the criminal himself is a victim of the social conditions that breed crime.' No one expects such an argument to result in a revised, rational code of criminal justice,'' he remarked, but, ''It does help each disputant to feel that he is on the side of the victim, which is, of course, the 'right' side. Unfortunatley,'' he concluded, ''it is no help to the judge.''

Wriston, drawing upon Arnold's concept, sagaciously observed:

In an American election year, polar words float on the horizon like the aurora borealis. They then subside, but never vanish. Nor should we want them to. Such words do, after all, have power to inspire. They provide focal points around which like-minded citizens can rally. They motivate change and social progress. We would do well to remember, however, that polar words are never guides to reasonable solutions or rational goals. They can make us want to move, but never tell us where we ought to go. For this we need a different kind of dialogue.

He reminded, also, of the power and pitfall of words in recounting the career of Antoine Lavoisier, the Father of Modern Chemistry. Wrote Lavoisier: ''Like three impressions of the same seal, the word ought to produce the idea, and the idea ought to be a picture of fact.'' Applying this principle to chemistry, Lavoisier compiled the dictionary that revolutionized the study of chemicals. Wriston then draws our attention to the fact that "... this event is often cited as proof of what clear and careful definition can accomplish." Yet, "It is unfortunate for the cause of clarity (as it was for him), that a few years later, when Lavoisier applied himself to politics, they cut off his head."

Despite these pitfalls in our language and logic, I am at one with Novak in decrying the decline of conformity to virtue in American society and with his call for a return to moral teaching. Should he lose his head for these judgments, I shall also lose mine. But, I suspect that we both, as does Wriston, see this call to build moral character and self-control primarily as a rallying point for change. For our concern is a matter of how and why virtue — if it is conformity to virtue and a particular form of it, law-abidingness, that is at stake — declines and whether and how moral character can be restored and moral concerns reinforced.

On these latter matters perhaps Mr. Novak and I may take somewhat different approaches. Mr. Novak seems more inclined than am I to see moral development as a property of each individual. People are free agents who exercise self-control over their behavior. I, as a sociologist, am wont to see conduct as a product of normative culture and of patterns of social control within a society — to see how a society develops normative and ethical standards and of how it then induces, reinforces, and complements moral behavior in people through self and social control. Likewise, I may be more content to focus more narrowly on how people come to behave in law-abiding ways and of how a society optimizes law-abidingness. And, although I am partial to a theory of normative life that sees norms that govern behavior as emergents of social control, i.e., norms arise when people deem it necessary to control behavior that they view as harmful to individual and collective interests, any norm, by itself, is not moral. For what makes behavior moral — another one of those polar words — is not the norm but an evaluation of the norm. That valuation — perhaps the conceptual equivalent of Adam Smith's money — has its source in cultures and their beliefs.

I was delighted to see, therefore, that at the outset Mr. Novak set the problem of crime in the context of an inquiry into the cause of virtue, "... keeping in view the *social* causes of the *social* virtues in *societies* taken as wholes." With that I was heartily in accord. It was of some concern, however, to discover that in his brilliant essay Mr. Novak's primary focus is largely on the defective character of persons and their personal responsibility for their criminal acts and that he regards committing a crime ordinarily a matter of personal choice and responsibility, a matter of self-control. I cannot altogether disagree. Nonetheless, to me, and I suspect also to him, the core question is how is one to account for these failures in self-control. Here our emphases are somewhat different, though not inherently contradictory. His answer lies primarily at the level of individuals, their families, and, to a lesser exent, their communities. Mine perhaps lies more at what causes societies to change their moral composition and concerns and their will to control behavior out of moral rather than instrumental interests. We are both, I think, interested finally in understanding not only the root causes of the decline in virtue, and hence of crime or law-abidingness, but of how we may cause law-abidingness. The causes of decline are not always the same as those of becoming.

Before exploring a bit further the root causes of the decline in virtue and of what we may need to know to restore it, I want to share with you a few troubling observations about changes in crime rates that we must bear in mind in seeking its root causes. All of these seem to be characteristic of Western post-industrial societies.

Perhaps the most striking thing about crime rates is how much lower they are among girls than boys and women than men. Although this gap may be narrowing, and there is considerable variation among the types of crime, the sex difference remains substantial. If men are less virtuous, why is that so?

Almost equally striking is the considerable variation in the crime rate of communities, both by neighborhoods within cities and among them. How much of this can we account for by differences in discipline and self-control or what, if any, other explanations do we have for it?

If we concentrate upon the most serious crimes, another troublesome fact — best documented for our society — is that during the period our crime rate was rising, there does not seem to have been a change in the prevalence of violators for crimes measured by the FBI Uniform Crime Index. That is to say, during this period of time the proportion of persons who commit one or more of these Index crimes has changed very little, if at all. The reason for the increase in these crimes seems to lie in the increased rate of offending among those who commit them, since we know there is considerable variation among persons in the rate at which they commit crimes. How are we to account for these changes in individual rates of offending?

Finally, and of this we may be less certain, there may be an increase in both the prevalence and incidence of offending for what are characterized as less serious crimes, and perhaps more so among the well-off than among the less affluent. Why is that taking place and what does that answer tell us about the virtue of nations? These changes may be more consequential for the virtue of nations than we ordinarily assume. Yet, we do not take seriously even their measurement.

Let me say something about these troubling facts in returning to our mutual inquiry into the virtue of nations. I explore first the question: Is there something about American society and its culture that makes it less virtuous — more crime prone — than many other nations? Why, for example, are people in our country more given to violence towards one another or less likely to practice peaceful relations and respect for one another? Why are we more given to theft and deceit, to murder and sexual assault, and to aggravated assault? Mr. Novak's answer is a precipitous decline in ethical culture, great historical events that undermined regard for virtues, such as the spread of liberal values, the cult of self-expression, and civil liberties, and a decline in discipline. These are not unimportant sources. Yet, this view scants the role that the changing culture and organization of society and its systems of social control have in undermining virtue and discipline.

The maintenance of self-control is part and parcel of social control. Declines in social control, in my view, lie at the root of a decline in self-control. Without external reinforcement, self-control not only fails to develop but it withers and decays. What seems to have taken place in American society is a decline in the reinforcement of moral norms and disciplining others in everyday life. One is no longer expected to be accountable for the moral life of others, to discipline children whether or not they are ours, and to bring them to virtue. We seem to have lost both the moral and organizational means for doing so — in families, in schools, in communities, and in public life generally. Especially noteworthy is the substitution of primary for secondary group controls. Equally noteworthy, perhaps, is a decline in local government and control by local institutions and the substitution of large-scale organizations and mass control.

We may turn to the nature of our culture and what it legitimates for some of the root causes. We are in this country an amalgam of many cultures, and there often is an uneasy truce over moral values. We seem to have forged a common culture based on a minimum consensus over moral matters — one that bargains for a minimum of behavior rather than conformity to moral ideals. Our culture and our formal agencies of control legitimate violence in myriad ways. A hockey match, for example, is often little more than a series of aggravated assaults for which the merest of penalties are given by those responsible for insuring the rules of the game are kept. Our public prosecutors and courts refuse to regard such assaults as aggravated and subject to criminal penalties. Why so? Are they not moral matters?

Remarkable also, is that a society of virtuous people can collectively engage in violence and harmful behavior towards others. The nineteenth century was surely not a time in which the collectivity could be proud of what it was doing. The history of the American Indian is indeed a sorry one — a history of frontier people and increasingly their government believing they might not only take the native's lands but of support for endeavors to replace their culture with one deemed vastly superior. Even the role of missionaries in that movement was not always one that could be justified on moral grounds, or at least so it appeared to many Indians. The Indians, not surprisingly, regarded the practices rather than the beliefs of the white man as the more symptomatic of what their god was like. It is also the period in which men of virtue enslaved others who were considered little more than savages — to be regarded as chattel. For much of the century and until quite recently, so were women regarded as less than men. More recently we have seen a government and a country divided over whether we should engage in wars against alien ideals in alien lands and whether it is moral for the State to punish by taking lives. Beyond that we seem to go through periods when men in high office behave badly out of political motives. Watergate is surely something to be put behind rather than before us. Additionally, the moral conduct of organizations and their employees is problematic. Such moral dilemmas are not easily resolved in a pluralistic culture and society. Homogeneity as well as heterogeneity has its virtues.

One might make a case that low crime rate societies and virtuous ones need not be rural communities or small societies. It should trouble most Americans that not only smaller Western nations like England, the Scandinavian countries, Holland, and West Germany have crime rates that are much lower than ours, but that a highly industrialized society such as Japan has an even lower crime rate.

Time does not permit me to do more than note the sharp cultural contrasts between American and Japanese societies in their emphasis on virtues. Japan has a homogeneous culture with core values of filial piety and service to others. Individual choice is replaced by duty to others. Thus, families, corporations, and indeed one's government are responsible for one's welfare and protection as one, in turn, is responsible for theirs. People are closely bound together not only morally and ethically but socially in a system of mutual claims and obligations. Can one imagine an American executive assuming moral responsiblility for an accident that took more than a hundred lives and doing so by committing suicide to redeem his family from the shame his failure brought them? Or, can we imagine an American airline company moving quickly without litigation to compensate families of those victims? Both of these occurred in Japan in a 1985 JAL disaster.

One cannot dismiss lightly the facts that even when Asians emigrated to the United States, their strong family and community structure remained relatively intact. Asian Americans have always had the lowest delinquency and crime rates of any ethnic minority in our cities. Does this suggest that their culture and social organization insulates them against the mass changes to which others have been so vulnerable?

One matter I find missing in Mr. Novak's exposition is how one builds a sense of moral obligation that binds people to one another so that they do no harm to one another and place the welfare of others above their own. For, at the core of all crime is a harming of others, a disregard, as Novak says, for the humanity of people. Perhaps individuals will lack that sense when there is too little emphasis on collective as well as individual responsibility for the welfare of others — a sense that others matter.

Where much crime is concentrated in our country, we allow, for example, deplorable housing conditions — conditions that almost no advanced industrial society permits. We might perhaps look at what that says about our regard for others and their dignity.

I do not know the answer to how much difference culture and social control make in the virtue of nations. But, as a social scientist, I think the evidence is quite clear that virtue is not enough. For part of the answer appears to lie in a society's culture and how it is structured and organized to control the behavior of others.

Perhaps one of the proximate causes of changing crime rates of individuals is to be found in how the very structure and organization of the American Society has changed in ways that make less possible the kind of moral socialization Mr. Novak describes and the kind of control I regard as necessary. Perhaps no single change is as dramatic as the shift in family structure. At least one-third of our children nowadays grow up in single family households. That household is usually headed by a woman who typically is the principal role model and disciplinarian for both male and female children. Often she works as well. Most black mothers in America must do so and have done so for a long time. What is changing also is the concentration of such households in communities — our crime-ridden communities.

The female headed household appears to be particularly devastating for the moral socialization of male youth. Lacking a male as a principal disciplinarian, they may well be less likely to develop that internal discipline Mr. Novak and I regard as essential to conformity to virtue. Moreover, with a mother absent at work and less resourceful in disciplining them, they take to the streets where there is an ample supply of similarly situated males. Peer discipline replaces parental discipline and the instrumental values of peers substitute for adult moral values. Additionally, their schools often are little more than blackboard jungles where internal discipline is difficult to maintain without the backing of parental authority and control, where learning is retarded by frequent truancy which families are unable to control, and where the school makes little effort to inculcate and reinforce moral values essential to moral self-discipline.

The single parent household in these communities may also have a deleterious impact on the moral socialization and control of female as well as male children. Their primary contacts in their teens are the male youths in these communities. Early pregnancy and a child born outside of wedlock are valued and a cycle of the single parent household begins anew.

It is not the single parent household per se but their concentration in some communities that appears to engender high crime rate communities and high rates of individual offending. One of the striking findings of recent research on communities and their crime rates explains why communities often move within less than a decade from a low to a high crime rate. This change is attributable in many cases to changes in the population composition of neighborhoods and communities so that they become disproportionally made up of single parent households and single transients. These changes in composition are attributable to a number of factors, but particularly to changes in the housing stock and public housing policies that concentrate low income single persons and single parent households in the same neighborhoods. As the male children in these households mature into adolescence, soft-crimes such as vandalism, petty theft, loitering, and littering become endemic. Stable families and businesses move out with this increase in soft-crime since they are increasingly vulnerable to their losses. When these male youths move through the teens, they begin to commit more serious offenses. Serious crime becomes endemic in these neighborhoods. Not only is family control weak in the single adult household, but adult community control becomes weak and ineffectual as local institutions and organizations disappear. The resident population consequently has few conventional ties to one another and few means of informally controlling criminal activity.

Such changes in neighborhoods are not inevitable but intervention is problematic in our society. If one is to intervene in this cycle of community change, one must intervene in ways that avoid these concentrations of single parent households and single transients. I am inclined to speculate that enforcement of the housing code to insure the quality of housing and of occupancy standards might do more to affect the crime rate in these neighborhoods than would increasing the numbers of police.

This densification of young males from single parent households in the same neighborhoods may also account for some of the increase in individual crime rates. The clumping of delinquent males and their consequent participation in delinquency in groups enhances the rate at which each individual commits offenses. These communities, moreover, become havens for drug dealing and recruitment of the young into substance abuse. Users, in turn, support their habit by increased crime. The individual crime rates of low income drug users are among the highest of any criminal offender rates. Wolfgang reports that the age of arrest for drug use among juveniles has been dropping. Consequently, higher individual rates of offending are probably developing at younger ages.

The foregoing is not intended to dismiss the significant and persuasive argument Mr. Novak advances about how the decline in discipline that leads to a weak moral character structure and diminished self-control has implications for crime rates. That this weakening is linked to changes in mass culture and social organization, there seems little doubt. That the decline is also profoundly linked to changes in family and local community organization and control likewise is apparent. One wonders, however, whether the decline in discipline and self-control has not had its greatest impact on soft rather than serious crime. And, perhaps it has had a particularly noticeable impact on the conduct of well-off youth. One might hazard the guess that the most profound consequence of the changes Mr. Novak has outlined is that they have made all social classes equally vulnerable. The effect of these trends and their continuation may be most pronounced on middle class delinquency and adult crime.

I conclude by emphasizing again that I find Mr. Novak's thesis not only brilliantly set forth but persuasive. If we want to reduce the volume of crime in the United States, we must seriously consider how we can develop and reinforce moral character and self-control. My remarks are intended to broaden the scope of that effort by looking to aspects of American culture and its social organization and control that are conducive to increasing conformity and which, in turn, are linked to character development and self-control. I have done so not only because I have been concerned with how to bring down the crime rate from its recent high but because I think that among the civilized nations of the world, even when we view our crime rate as low, it seems intolerably high.

This judgment signals not only a call to return to past virtue but to become more virtuous. In becoming more virtuous, we perhaps shall not only care more for the welfare of ourselves but for the welfare of others. We shall feel responsible not only for what we do but for what others do as well.

And, is it too much to expect that we may also become more concerned for the morality of our collective as well as for our individual acts? Or, that we may aspire to — though we may never achieve — that form of altruism envisioned by St. Augustine and *The City of God*?